MznLnx

Missing Links Exam Preps

Exam Prep for

Calculus for Business, Economics, Life Sciences, and Social Sciences

Barnett & Ziegler & Byleen, 9th Edition

The MznLnx Exam Prep is your link from the texbook and lecture to your exams.
The MznLnx Exam Preps are unauthorized and comprehensive reviews of your textbooks.

All material provided by MznLnx and Rico Publications (c) 2010
Textbook publishers and textbook authors do not particpate in or contribute to these reviews.

MznLnx

Rico
Publications

Exam Prep for Calculus for Business, Economics, Life Sciences, and Social Sciences
9th Edition
Barnett & Ziegler & Byleen

Publisher: Raymond Houge
Assistant Editor: Michael Rouger
Text and Cover Designer: Lisa Buckner
Marketing Manager: Sara Swagger
Project Manager, Editorial Production: Jerry Emerson
Art Director: Vernon Lowerui

Product Manager: Dave Mason
Editorial Assitant: Rachel Guzmanji
Pedagogy: Debra Long
Cover Image: Jim Reed/Getty Images
Text and Cover Printer: City Printing, Inc.
Compositor: Media Mix, Inc.

(c) 2010 Rico Publications
ALL RIGHTS RESERVED. No part of this work covered by the copyright may be reproduced or used in any form or by an means--graphic, electronic, or mechanical, including photocopying, recording, taping, Web distribution, information storage, and retrieval systems, or in any other manner--without the written permission of the publisher.

Printed in the United States
ISBN:

For more information about our products, contact us at:
Dave.Mason@RicoPublications.com

For permission to use material from this text or product, submit a request online to:
Dave.Mason@RicoPublications.com

Contents

CHAPTER 1
A Beginning Library of Elementary Functions — 1

CHAPTER 2
Additional Elementary Functions — 11

CHAPTER 3
The Derivative — 25

CHAPTER 4
Graphing and Optimization — 39

CHAPTER 5
Additional Derivative Topics — 54

CHAPTER 6
Integration — 65

CHAPTER 7
Additional Integration Topics — 80

CHAPTER 8
Multivariable Calculus — 89

CHAPTER 9
Trigonometric Functions — 104

ANSWER KEY — 114

TO THE STUDENT

COMPREHENSIVE

The *MznLnx* Exam Prep series is designed to help you pass your exams. Editors at MznLnx review your textbooks and then prepare these practice exams to help you master the textbook material. Unlike study guides, workbooks, and practice tests provided by the texbook publisher and textbook authors, *MznLnx* gives you **all** of the material in each chapter in exam form, not just samples, so you can be sure to nail your exam.

MECHANICAL

The MznLnx Exam Prep series creates exams that will help you learn the subject matter as well as test you on your understanding. Each question is designed to help you master the concept. Just working through the exams, you gain an understanding of the subject--its a simple mechanical process that produces success.

INTEGRATED STUDY GUIDE AND REVIEW

MznLnx is not just a set of exams designed to test you, its also a comprehensive review of the subject content. Each exam question is also a review of the concept, making sure that you will get the answer correct without having to go to other sources of material. You learn as you go! Its the easiest way to pass an exam.

HUMOR

Studying can be tedious and dry. MznLnx's instructional design includes moderate humor within the exam questions on occassion, to break the tedium and revitalize the brain

Chapter 1. A Beginning Library of Elementary Functions 1

1. _____ are the basic objects of study in graph theory. Informally speaking, a graph is a set of objects called points, nodes, or vertices connected by links called lines or edges.
   a. Thing
   b. Graphs0
   c. Undefined
   d. Undefined

2. The mathematical concept of a _____ expresses the intuitive idea of deterministic dependence between two quantities, one of which is viewed as primary and the other as secondary. A _____ then is a way to associate a unique output for each input of a specified type, for example, a real number or an element of a given set.
   a. Thing
   b. Function0
   c. Undefined
   d. Undefined

3. An _____ is a straight line around which a geometric figure can be rotated.
   a. Thing
   b. Axis0
   c. Undefined
   d. Undefined

4. In astronomy, geography, geometry and related sciences and contexts, a plane is said to be _____ at a given point if it is locally perpendicular to the gradient of the gravity field, i.e., with the direction of the gravitational force at that point.
   a. Thing
   b. Horizontal0
   c. Undefined
   d. Undefined

5. A _____ consists of one quarter of the coordinate plane.
   a. Thing
   b. Quadrant0
   c. Undefined
   d. Undefined

6. An _____ is when two lines intersect somewhere on a plane creating a right angle at intersection
   a. Axes0
   b. Thing
   c. Undefined
   d. Undefined

7. In mathematics, a _____ is a two-dimensional manifold or surface that is perfectly flat.
   a. Plane0
   b. Thing
   c. Undefined
   d. Undefined

8. A _____ is a set of numbers that designate location in a given reference system, such as x,y in a planar _____ system or an x,y,z in a three-dimensional _____ system.
   a. Coordinate0
   b. Thing
   c. Undefined
   d. Undefined

9. In mathematics and its applications, a _____ is a system for assigning an n-tuple of numbers or scalars to each point in an n-dimensional space.
   a. Coordinate system0
   b. Concept
   c. Undefined
   d. Undefined

10. In mathematics, the _____ of a coordinate system is the point where the axes of the system intersect.
    a. Thing
    b. Origin0
    c. Undefined
    d. Undefined

11. _____ means of or relating to the French philosopher and mathematician René Descartes.

Chapter 1. A Beginning Library of Elementary Functions

    a. Thing
    c. Undefined
    b. Cartesian0
    d. Undefined

12. In mathematics, a _____ may be described informally as a number that can be given by an infinite decimal representation.
    a. Thing
    b. Real number0
    c. Undefined
    d. Undefined

13. An _____ is a collection of two not necessarily distinct objects, one of which is distinguished as the first coordinate and the other as the second coordinate.
    a. Thing
    b. Ordered pair0
    c. Undefined
    d. Undefined

14. _____ is the study of geometry using the principles of algebra. _____ can be explained more simply: it is concerned with defining geometrical shapes in a numerical way and extracting numerical information from that representation.
    a. Thing
    b. Analytic geometry0
    c. Undefined
    d. Undefined

15. In mathematics, a _____ is a statement that can be proved on the basis of explicitly stated or previously agreed assumptions.
    a. Theorem0
    b. Thing
    c. Undefined
    d. Undefined

16. In number theory, the _____ of arithmetic (or unique factorization theorem) states that every natural number greater than 1 can be written as a unique product of prime numbers.
    a. Concept
    b. Fundamental theorem0
    c. Undefined
    d. Undefined

17. An _____ or member of a set is an object that when collected together make up the set.
    a. Element0
    b. Thing
    c. Undefined
    d. Undefined

18. In mathematics, the _____ , or members of a set or more generally a class are all those objects which when collected together make up the set or class.
    a. Elements0
    b. Thing
    c. Undefined
    d. Undefined

19. A _____ is a set of possible values that a variable can take on in order to satisfy a given set of conditions, which may include equations and inequalities.
    a. Solution set0
    b. Thing
    c. Undefined
    d. Undefined

20. _____ is the state of being greater than any finite real or natural number, however large.

a. Thing
c. Undefined
b. Infinite0
d. Undefined

21. In mathematics, the conjugate _____ or adjoint matrix of an m-by-n matrix A with complex entries is the n-by-m matrix A* obtained from A by taking the transpose and then taking the complex conjugate of each entry.
   a. Pairs0
   b. Thing
   c. Undefined
   d. Undefined

22. In mathematics, the concept of a _____ tries to capture the intuitive idea of a geometrical one-dimensional and continuous object. A simple example is the circle.
   a. Curve0
   b. Thing
   c. Undefined
   d. Undefined

23. In mathematics, the _____ is a conic section generated by the intersection of a right circular conical surface and a plane parallel to a generating straight line of that surface. It can also be defined as locus of points in a plane which are equidistant from a given point.
   a. Parabola0
   b. Thing
   c. Undefined
   d. Undefined

24. _____ is an adjective usually refering to being in the centre.
   a. Thing
   b. Central0
   c. Undefined
   d. Undefined

25. In mathematics, an _____, mean, or central tendency of a data set refers to a measure of the "middle" or "expected" value of the data set.
   a. Average0
   b. Concept
   c. Undefined
   d. Undefined

26. _____ is a physical property of a system that underlies the common notions of hot and cold; something that is hotter has the greater _____.
   a. Thing
   b. Temperature0
   c. Undefined
   d. Undefined

27. A _____ is a statement or claimt that a particular event will occur in the future in more certain terms than a forecast.
   a. Prediction0
   b. Thing
   c. Undefined
   d. Undefined

28. _____ is the application of tools and a processing medium to the transformation of raw materials into finished goods for sale.
   a. Manufacturing0
   b. Thing
   c. Undefined
   d. Undefined

29. In mathematics, the _____ of a function is the set of all "output" values produced by that function. Given a function $f : A \to B$, the _____ of f, is defined to be the set $\{x \in B : x = f(a) \text{ for some } a \in A\}$.

Chapter 1. A Beginning Library of Elementary Functions

a. Thing
c. Undefined

b. Range0
d. Undefined

30. In mathematics, a _____ of a k-place relation $L \subseteq X_1 \times ... \times X_k$ is one of the sets X_j, $1 \leq j \leq k$. In the special case where k = 2 and $L \subseteq X_1 \times X_2$ is a function $L : X_1 \to X_2$, it is conventional to refer to X_1 as the _____ of the function and to refer to X_2 as the codomain of the function.

a. Domain0
c. Undefined

b. Thing
d. Undefined

31. A _____ is a symbolic representation denoting a quantity or expression. It often represents an "unknown" quantity that has the potential to change.

a. Thing
c. Undefined

b. Variable0
d. Undefined

32. In mathematics, an _____ is any of the arguments, i.e. "inputs", to a function. Thus if we have a function f(x), then x is a _____.

a. Thing
c. Undefined

b. Independent variable0
d. Undefined

33. In a function the _____, is the variable which is the value, i.e. the "output", of the function.

a. Thing
c. Undefined

b. Dependent variable0
d. Undefined

34. In plane geometry, a _____ is a polygon with four equal sides, four right angles, and parallel opposite sides. In algebra, the _____ of a number is that number multiplied by itself.

a. Square0
c. Undefined

b. Thing
d. Undefined

35. In mathematics, a _____ of a number x is a number r such that $r^2 = x$, or in words, a number r whose square (the result of multiplying the number by itself) is x.

a. Square root0
c. Undefined

b. Thing
d. Undefined

36. In mathematics, a _____ of a complex-valued function f is a member x of the domain of f such that f(x) vanishes at x, that is, $x : f(x) = 0$.

a. Root0
c. Undefined

b. Thing
d. Undefined

37. In mathematics, an inequality is a statement about the relative size or order of two objects. For example 14 > 10, or 14 is _____ 10.

a. Thing
c. Undefined

b. Greater than0
d. Undefined

38. Mathematical _____ is used to represent ideas.

Chapter 1. A Beginning Library of Elementary Functions 5

a. Thing
b. Notation0
c. Undefined
d. Undefined

39. In mathematics, an _____ is a statement about the relative size or order of two objects.
a. Thing
b. Inequality0
c. Undefined
d. Undefined

40. In elementary algebra, an _____ is a set that contains every real number between two indicated numbers and may contain the two numbers themselves.
a. Thing
b. Interval0
c. Undefined
d. Undefined

41. _____ is the notation in which permitted values for a variable are expressed as ranging over a certain interval; "5 < x < 9" is an example of the application of _____.
a. Thing
b. Interval notation0
c. Undefined
d. Undefined

42. In mathematics, a _____ is the result of multiplying, or an expression that identifies factors to be multiplied.
a. Thing
b. Product0
c. Undefined
d. Undefined

43. An _____ is a combination of numbers, operators, grouping symbols and/or free variables and bound variables arranged in a meaningful way which can be evaluated..
a. Expression0
b. Thing
c. Undefined
d. Undefined

44. _____, from Latin meaning "to make progress", is defined in two different ways. Pure economic _____ is the increase in wealth that an investor has from making an investment, taking into consideration all costs associated with that investment including the opportunity cost of capital.
a. Profit0
b. Thing
c. Undefined
d. Undefined

45. _____ is a synonym for information.
a. Thing
b. Data0
c. Undefined
d. Undefined

46. _____ is the part of statistical practice concerned with the selection of individual observations intended to yield some knowledge about a population of concern, especially for the purposes of statistical inference.
a. Thing
b. Sampling0
c. Undefined
d. Undefined

47. In economics, supply and _____ describe market relations between prospective sellers and buyers of a good.
a. Thing
b. Demand0
c. Undefined
d. Undefined

Chapter 1. A Beginning Library of Elementary Functions

48. _____ is a business term for the amount of money that a company receives from its activities in a given period, mostly from sales of products and/or services to customers
   a. Revenue0
   b. Thing
   c. Undefined
   d. Undefined

49. According to the United Nations Statistics Division, _____ is the resale sale without transformation of new and used goods to retailers, to industrial, commercial, institutional or professional users, or to other wholesalers, or involves acting as an agent or broker in buying merchandise for, or selling merchandise, to such persons or companies.
   a. Wholesale0
   b. Thing
   c. Undefined
   d. Undefined

50. In common philosophical language, a proposition or _____, is the content of an assertion, that is, it is true-or-false and defined by the meaning of a particular piece of language.
   a. Statement0
   b. Concept
   c. Undefined
   d. Undefined

51. A _____ is a three-dimensional solid object bounded by six square faces, facets, or sides, with three meeting at each vertex.
   a. Thing
   b. Cube0
   c. Undefined
   d. Undefined

52. In geometry, a _____ is defined as a quadrilateral where all four of its angles are right angles.
   a. Thing
   b. Rectangle0
   c. Undefined
   d. Undefined

53. _____ is the distance around a given two-dimensional object. As a general rule, the _____ of a polygon can always be calculated by adding all the length of the sides together. So, the formula for triangles is P = a + b + c, where a, b and c stand for each side of it. For quadrilaterals the equation is P = a + b + c + d. For equilateral polygons, P = na, where n is the number of sides and a is the side length.
   a. Perimeter0
   b. Thing
   c. Undefined
   d. Undefined

54. The _____ of measurement are a globally standardized and modernized form of the metric system.
   a. Thing
   b. Units0
   c. Undefined
   d. Undefined

55. A _____ is a function that assigns a number to subsets of a given set.
   a. Measure0
   b. Thing
   c. Undefined
   d. Undefined

56. The _____ of a solid object is the three-dimensional concept of how much space it occupies, often quantified numerically.
   a. Volume0
   b. Thing
   c. Undefined
   d. Undefined

57. In Euclidean geometry, a _____ is moving every point a constant distance in a specified direction.

Chapter 1. A Beginning Library of Elementary Functions

    a. Translation0   b. Concept
    c. Undefined   d. Undefined

58. A _____ is a number that is less than zero.
    a. Negative number0   b. Thing
    c. Undefined   d. Undefined

59. In mathematics, a _____ (also spelled reflexion) is a map that transforms an object into its mirror image.
    a. Concept   b. Reflection0
    c. Undefined   d. Undefined

60. In combinatorial mathematics, a _____ is an un-ordered collection of unique elements.
    a. Combination0   b. Concept
    c. Undefined   d. Undefined

61. An _____ of a product of sums expresses it as a sum of products by using the fact that multiplication distributes over addition.
    a. Thing   b. Expansion0
    c. Undefined   d. Undefined

62. The _____ is the y- coordinate of a point within a two dimensional coordinate system. It is sometimes used to refer to the axis rather than the distance along the coordinate system.
    a. Thing   b. Ordinate0
    c. Undefined   d. Undefined

63. In a mathematical proof or a syllogism, a _____ is a statement that is the logical consequence of preceding statements.
    a. Concept   b. Conclusion0
    c. Undefined   d. Undefined

64. In mathematics and the mathematical sciences, a _____ is a fixed, but possibly unspecified, value. This is in contrast to a variable, which is not fixed.
    a. Constant0   b. Thing
    c. Undefined   d. Undefined

65. In mathematics, a _____ in elementary terms is any of a variety of different functions from geometry, such as rotations, reflections and translations.
    a. Transformation0   b. Thing
    c. Undefined   d. Undefined

66. A _____ defined function $f(x)$ of a real variable x is a function whose definition is given differently on disjoint subsets of its domain.
    a. Thing   b. Piecewise0
    c. Undefined   d. Undefined

67. In mathematics, the _____ (or modulus) of a real number is its numerical value without regard to its sign.

a. Absolute value0
c. Undefined
b. Thing
d. Undefined

68. In mathematics, _____ geometry was the traditional name for the geometry of three-dimensional Euclidean space — for practical purposes the kind of space we live in.
   a. Thing
   b. Solid0
   c. Undefined
   d. Undefined

69. A _____ is a negotiable instrument instructing a financial institution to pay a specific amount of a specific currency from a specific demand account held in the maker/depositor's name with that institution. Both the maker and payee may be natural persons or legal entities.
   a. Check0
   b. Thing
   c. Undefined
   d. Undefined

70. In mathematics, a _____ is an ordered list of objects. Like a set, it contains members, also called elements or terms, and the number of terms is called the length of the _____. Unlike a set, order matters, and the exact same elements can appear multiple times at different positions in the _____.
   a. Thing
   b. Sequence0
   c. Undefined
   d. Undefined

71. A _____ is a special kind of ratio, indicating a relationship between two measurements with different units, such as miles to gallons or cents to pounds.
   a. Rate0
   b. Thing
   c. Undefined
   d. Undefined

72. _____ is the portion of income that is the subject of taxation according to the laws that determine what is income and the taxation rate for that income.
   a. Taxable income0
   b. Thing
   c. Undefined
   d. Undefined

73. The metre (or _____, see spelling differences) is a measure of length. It is the basic unit of length in the metric system and in the International System of Units (SI), used around the world for general and scientific purposes.
   a. Meter0
   b. Concept
   c. Undefined
   d. Undefined

74. A _____ is a unit of length, usually used to measure distance, in a number of different systems, including Imperial units, United States customary units and Norwegian/Swedish mil. Its size can vary from system to system, but in each is between 1 and 10 kilometers. In contemporary English contexts _____ refers to either:
   a. Thing
   b. Mile0
   c. Undefined
   d. Undefined

75. _____ is a unit of speed, expressing the number of international miles covered per hour.
   a. Miles per hour0
   b. Thing
   c. Undefined
   d. Undefined

76. Any point where a graph makes contact with an coordinate axis is called an _____ of the graph

Chapter 1. A Beginning Library of Elementary Functions 9

   a. Thing
   b. Intercept0
   c. Undefined
   d. Undefined

77. In mathematics, the _____ f is the collection of all ordered pairs . In particular, graph means the graphical representation of this collection, in the form of a curve or surface, together with axes, etc. Graphing on a Cartesian plane is sometimes referred to as curve sketching.
   a. Thing
   b. Graph of a function0
   c. Undefined
   d. Undefined

78. The word _____ comes from the Latin word linearis, which means created by lines.
   a. Linear0
   b. Thing
   c. Undefined
   d. Undefined

79. A _____ is a first degree polynomial mathematical function of the form: f(x) = mx + b where m and b are real constants and x is a real variable.
   a. Thing
   b. Linear function0
   c. Undefined
   d. Undefined

80. _____ is a function whose values do not vary and thus are constant.
   a. Constant function0
   b. Thing
   c. Undefined
   d. Undefined

81. In mathematics, a _____ is an expression that is constructed from one or more variables and constants, using only the operations of addition, subtraction, multiplication, and constant positive whole number exponents. is a _____. Note in particular that division by an expression containing a variable is not in general allowed in polynomials. [1]
   a. Polynomial0
   b. Thing
   c. Undefined
   d. Undefined

82. An _____ is an equality that remains true regardless of the values of any variables that appear within it, to distinguish it from an equality which is true under more particular conditions.
   a. Thing
   b. Identity0
   c. Undefined
   d. Undefined

83. An _____ is a function that does not have any effect: it always returns the same value that was used as its argument.
   a. Identity function0
   b. Thing
   c. Undefined
   d. Undefined

84. In linear algebra, the _____ of an n-by-n square matrix A is defined to be the sum of the elements on the main diagonal of A,
   a. Thing
   b. Trace0
   c. Undefined
   d. Undefined

85. A _____ is a tool similar to a ruler, but without markings.

Chapter 1. A Beginning Library of Elementary Functions

    a. Thing
    b. Straightedge0
    c. Undefined
    d. Undefined

86. A _____ is a quantity that denotes the proportional amount or magnitude of one quantity relative to another.
    a. Thing
    b. Ratio0
    c. Undefined
    d. Undefined

87. _____ is often used to describe the measurement of the steepness, incline, gradient, or grade of a straight line. The _____ is defined as the ratio of the "rise" divided by the "run" between two points on a line, or in other words, the ratio of the altitude change to the horizontal distance between any two points on the line.
    a. Thing
    b. Slope0
    c. Undefined
    d. Undefined

88. _____ is a regression method that models the relationship between a dependent variable Y, independent variables X_p, and a random term å.
    a. Linear regression0
    b. Thing
    c. Undefined
    d. Undefined

89. _____ the expected value of a random variable displays the average or central value of the variable. It is a summary value of the distribution of the variable.
    a. Determining0
    b. Thing
    c. Undefined
    d. Undefined

90. In mathematics, a _____ is a constant multiplicative factor of a certain object. The object can be such things as a variable, a vector, a function, etc. For example, the _____ of $9x^2$ is 9.
    a. Coefficient0
    b. Thing
    c. Undefined
    d. Undefined

91. A _____ is a landform that extends above the surrounding terrain in a limited area. A _____ is generally steeper than a hill, but there is no universally accepted standard definition for the height of a _____ or a hill although a _____ usually has an identifiable summit.
    a. Thing
    b. Mountain0
    c. Undefined
    d. Undefined

92. A _____ is an abstract model that uses mathematical language to describe the behavior of a system. Eykhoff defined a _____ as 'a representation of the essential aspects of an existing system which presents knowledge of that system in usable form'.
    a. Mathematical model0
    b. Thing
    c. Undefined
    d. Undefined

Chapter 2. Additional Elementary Functions

1. A _____ is a polynomial function of the form $f(x) = ax^2 + bx + c$, where a, b, c are real numbers and a , 0.
   a. Quadratic function0
   b. Event
   c. Undefined
   d. Undefined

2. The word _____ comes from the Latin word linearis, which means created by lines.
   a. Thing
   b. Linear0
   c. Undefined
   d. Undefined

3. In mathematics, a _____ is an expression that is constructed from one or more variables and constants, using only the operations of addition, subtraction, multiplication, and constant positive whole number exponents. is a _____. Note in particular that division by an expression containing a variable is not in general allowed in polynomials. [1]
   a. Polynomial0
   b. Thing
   c. Undefined
   d. Undefined

4. The mathematical concept of a _____ expresses the intuitive idea of deterministic dependence between two quantities, one of which is viewed as primary and the other as secondary. A _____ then is a way to associate a unique output for each input of a specified type, for example, a real number or an element of a given set.
   a. Function0
   b. Thing
   c. Undefined
   d. Undefined

5. The _____ integers are all the integers from zero on upwards.
   a. Thing
   b. Nonnegative0
   c. Undefined
   d. Undefined

6. In mathematics, a _____ may be described informally as a number that can be given by an infinite decimal representation.
   a. Real number0
   b. Thing
   c. Undefined
   d. Undefined

7. _____ is a function of the form
   a. Cubic function0
   b. Thing
   c. Undefined
   d. Undefined

8. In mathematics and the mathematical sciences, a _____ is a fixed, but possibly unspecified, value. This is in contrast to a variable, which is not fixed.
   a. Thing
   b. Constant0
   c. Undefined
   d. Undefined

9. _____ is a function whose values do not vary and thus are constant.
   a. Constant function0
   b. Thing
   c. Undefined
   d. Undefined

10. In mathematics, there are several meanings of _____ depending on the subject.
    a. Thing
    b. Degree0
    c. Undefined
    d. Undefined

Chapter 2. Additional Elementary Functions

11. In mathematics, a _____ of a k-place relation $L \subseteq X_1 \times ... \times X_k$ is one of the sets X_j, $1 \le j \le k$. In the special case where k = 2 and $L \subseteq X_1 \times X_2$ is a function $L : X_1 \to X_2$, it is conventional to refer to X_1 as the _____ of the function and to refer to X_2 as the codomain of the function.
    a. Domain0
    b. Thing
    c. Undefined
    d. Undefined

12. _____ are external two-dimensional outlines, with the appearance or configuration of some thing - in contrast to the matter or content or substance of which it is composed.
    a. Shapes0
    b. Thing
    c. Undefined
    d. Undefined

13. _____ are the basic objects of study in graph theory. Informally speaking, a graph is a set of objects called points, nodes, or vertices connected by links called lines or edges.
    a. Thing
    b. Graphs0
    c. Undefined
    d. Undefined

14. An _____ is a straight line around which a geometric figure can be rotated.
    a. Axis0
    b. Thing
    c. Undefined
    d. Undefined

15. In mathematics, a _____ is a constant multiplicative factor of a certain object. The object can be such things as a variable, a vector, a function, etc. For example, the _____ of $9x^2$ is 9.
    a. Coefficient0
    b. Thing
    c. Undefined
    d. Undefined

16. In mathematics, a _____ number is a number which can be expressed as a ratio of two integers. Non-integer _____ numbers (commonly called fractions) are usually written as the vulgar fraction a / b, where b is not zero.
    a. Thing
    b. Rational0
    c. Undefined
    d. Undefined

17. A _____ function is a function for which, intuitively, small changes in the input result in small changes in the output.
    a. Continuous0
    b. Event
    c. Undefined
    d. Undefined

18. Any point where a graph makes contact with an coordinate axis is called an _____ of the graph
    a. Intercept0
    b. Thing
    c. Undefined
    d. Undefined

19. In mathematics, a _____ of a complex-valued function f is a member x of the domain of f such that f(x) vanishes at x, that is, $x : f(x) = 0$.
    a. Root0
    b. Thing
    c. Undefined
    d. Undefined

20. In mathematics, a _____ is a statement that can be proved on the basis of explicitly stated or previously agreed assumptions.

Chapter 2. Additional Elementary Functions

a. Theorem0
b. Thing
c. Undefined
d. Undefined

21. _____ has many meanings, most of which simply .
    a. Thing
    b. Power0
    c. Undefined
    d. Undefined

22. A _____ is a first degree polynomial mathematical function of the form: f(x) = mx + b where m and b are real constants and x is a real variable.
    a. Linear function0
    b. Thing
    c. Undefined
    d. Undefined

23. In mathematics, the concept of a _____ tries to capture the intuitive idea of a geometrical one-dimensional and continuous object. A simple example is the circle.
    a. Curve0
    b. Thing
    c. Undefined
    d. Undefined

24. In mathematics, _____ are the intuitive idea of a geometrical one-dimensional and continuous object.
    a. Thing
    b. Curves0
    c. Undefined
    d. Undefined

25. _____ is a synonym for information.
    a. Data0
    b. Thing
    c. Undefined
    d. Undefined

26. The act of _____ is the calculated approximation of a result which is usable even if input data may be incomplete, uncertain, or noisy.
    a. Thing
    b. Estimating0
    c. Undefined
    d. Undefined

27. _____ is the fee paid on borrowed money.
    a. Thing
    b. Interest0
    c. Undefined
    d. Undefined

28. _____ is a regression method that models the relationship between a dependent variable Y, independent variables Xp, and a random term å.
    a. Thing
    b. Linear regression0
    c. Undefined
    d. Undefined

29. In mathematics, a _____ is the end result of a division problem. It can also be expressed as the number of times the divisor divides into the dividend.
    a. Quotient0
    b. Thing
    c. Undefined
    d. Undefined

30. In mathematics, a _____ is any function which can be written as the ratio of two polynomial functions.

Chapter 2. Additional Elementary Functions

    a. Rational function0
    c. Undefined
    b. Thing
    d. Undefined

31. In mathematics, a _____ is a number which can be expressed as a ratio of two integers. Non-integer rational numbers (commonly called fractions) are usually written as the vulgar fraction a / b, where b is not zero.
    a. Concept
    b. Rational Number0
    c. Undefined
    d. Undefined

32. The _____ are the only integral domain whose positive elements are well-ordered, and in which order is preserved by addition. Like the natural numbers, the _____ form a countably infinite set. The set of all _____ is usually denoted in mathematics by a boldface Z.
    a. Integers0
    b. Thing
    c. Undefined
    d. Undefined

33. A _____ is the part of a fraction that tells how many equal parts make up a whole, and which is used in the name of the fraction: "halves", "thirds", "fourths" or "quarters", "fifths" and so on.
    a. Denominator0
    b. Concept
    c. Undefined
    d. Undefined

34. The _____ of a ring R is defined to be the smallest positive integer n such that n a = 0, for all a in R.
    a. Thing
    b. Characteristic0
    c. Undefined
    d. Undefined

35. In geographic information systems, a _____ comprises an entity with a geographic location, typically determined by points, arcs, or polygons. Carriageways and cadastres exemplify _____ data.
    a. Feature0
    b. Thing
    c. Undefined
    d. Undefined

36. Continuous functions are of utmost importance in mathematics and applications. However, not all functions are continuous. If a function is not continuous at a point in its domain, one says that it has a _____ there. The set of all points of _____ of a function may be a discrete set, a dense set, or even the entire domain of the function.
    a. Thing
    b. Discontinuity0
    c. Undefined
    d. Undefined

37. _____ is a straight line or curve A to which another curve B the one being studied approaches closer and closer as one moves along it.
    a. Vertical asymptote0
    b. Thing
    c. Undefined
    d. Undefined

38. An _____ is a straight line or curve A to which another curve B approaches closer and closer as one moves along it. As one moves along B, the space between it and the _____ A becomes smaller and smaller, and can in fact be made as small as one could wish by going far enough along. A curve may or may not touch or cross its _____. In fact, the curve may intersect the _____ an infinite number of times.
    a. Thing
    b. Asymptote0
    c. Undefined
    d. Undefined

Chapter 2. Additional Elementary Functions

39. A _____ is a numeral used to indicate a count. The most common use of the word today is to name the part of a fraction that tells the number or count of equal parts.
   a. Thing
   b. Numerator0
   c. Undefined
   d. Undefined

40. In astronomy, geography, geometry and related sciences and contexts, a plane is said to be _____ at a given point if it is locally perpendicular to the gradient of the gravity field, i.e., with the direction of the gravitational force at that point.
   a. Horizontal0
   b. Thing
   c. Undefined
   d. Undefined

41. In mathematics, the _____ of a coordinate system is the point where the axes of the system intersect.
   a. Origin0
   b. Thing
   c. Undefined
   d. Undefined

42. In mathematics, an _____, mean, or central tendency of a data set refers to a measure of the "middle" or "expected" value of the data set.
   a. Average0
   b. Concept
   c. Undefined
   d. Undefined

43. In mathematics, in the field of group theory, a _____ of a group is a quasisimple subnormal subgroup.
   a. Component0
   b. Concept
   c. Undefined
   d. Undefined

44. In finance, a _____ is collateral that the holder of a position in securities, options, or futures contracts has to deposit to cover the credit risk of his counterparty.
   a. Margin0
   b. Thing
   c. Undefined
   d. Undefined

45. In mathematics, the _____ is a conic section generated by the intersection of a right circular conical surface and a plane parallel to a generating straight line of that surface. It can also be defined as locus of points in a plane which are equidistant from a given point.
   a. Parabola0
   b. Thing
   c. Undefined
   d. Undefined

46. _____ is the application of tools and a processing medium to the transformation of raw materials into finished goods for sale.
   a. Manufacturing0
   b. Thing
   c. Undefined
   d. Undefined

Chapter 2. Additional Elementary Functions

47. Fixed costs are expenses whose total does not change in proportion to the activity of a business.Unit fixed costs decline with volume following a retangular hyperbola as the volume of production.Variable costs by contrast change in relation to the activity of a business such as sales or production volume.Along with variable costs,fixed costs make up one of the two components of total cost. In the most simple production function total cost is equal to fixed costs plus variable costs.In accounting terminology, fixed costs will broadly include all costs which are not included in cost of goods sold, and variable costs are those captured in costs of goods sold. The implicit assumption required to make the equivalence between the accounting and economics terminology is that the accounting period is equal to the period in which fixed costs do not vary in relation to production. In practice, this equivalence does not always hold and depending on the period under consideration by management, some overhead expenses can be adjusted by management, and the specific allocation of each expense to each category will be decided under cost accounting.In business planning and management accounting, usage of the terms fixed costs, variable costs and others will often differ from usage in economics, and may depend on the intended use. For example, costs may be segregated into per unit costs fixed costs per period, and variable costs as a proportion of revenue. Capital expenditures will usually be allocated separately, and depending on the purpose, a portion may be regularly allocated to expenses as depreciation and amortization and seen as a _____ per period, or the entire amount may be considered upfront fixed costs.
    a. Fixed cost0
    b. Thing
    c. Undefined
    d. Undefined

48. _____ are expenses whose total does not change in proportion to the activity of a business, within the relevant time period or scale of production
    a. Fixed costs0
    b. Thing
    c. Undefined
    d. Undefined

49. Initial objects are also called _____, and terminal objects are also called final.
    a. Coterminal0
    b. Thing
    c. Undefined
    d. Undefined

50. In linear algebra, the _____ of an n-by-n square matrix A is defined to be the sum of the elements on the main diagonal of A,
    a. Thing
    b. Trace0
    c. Undefined
    d. Undefined

51. In economics, economic _____ is simply a state of the world where economic forces are balanced and in the absence of external influences the values of economic variables will not change.
    a. Equilibrium0
    b. Thing
    c. Undefined
    d. Undefined

52. _____ is the level of functional and/or metabolic efficiency of an organism at both the micro level.
    a. Health0
    b. Thing
    c. Undefined
    d. Undefined

53. _____ was a U.S. pioneer in the fields of psychometrics and psychophysics. He conceived the approach to measurement known as the law of comparative judgment, and is well known for his contributions to factor analysis.
    a. Person
    b. Thurstone0
    c. Undefined
    d. Undefined

Chapter 2. Additional Elementary Functions

54. In mathematics, _____ growth occurs when the growth rate of a function is always proportional to the function's current size.
    a. Thing
    b. Exponential0
    c. Undefined
    d. Undefined

55. _____ is one of the most important functions in mathematics. A function commonly used to study growth and decay
    a. Exponential function0
    b. Thing
    c. Undefined
    d. Undefined

56. A _____ is a symbolic representation denoting a quantity or expression. It often represents an "unknown" quantity that has the potential to change.
    a. Thing
    b. Variable0
    c. Undefined
    d. Undefined

57. In mathematics, the _____ of a function is the set of all "output" values produced by that function. Given a function $f : A \to B$, the _____ of f, is defined to be the set $\{x \in B : x = f(a) \text{ for some } a \in A\}$.
    a. Range0
    b. Thing
    c. Undefined
    d. Undefined

58. A _____ is a special kind of ratio, indicating a relationship between two measurements with different units, such as miles to gallons or cents to pounds.
    a. Rate0
    b. Thing
    c. Undefined
    d. Undefined

59. A _____ is a set of numbers that designate location in a given reference system, such as x,y in a planar _____ system or an x,y,z in a three-dimensional _____ system.
    a. Thing
    b. Coordinate0
    c. Undefined
    d. Undefined

60. An _____ is when two lines intersect somewhere on a plane creating a right angle at intersection
    a. Thing
    b. Axes0
    c. Undefined
    d. Undefined

61. _____ is a set of numbers, in the broadest sense of the word, together with one or more operations, such as addition or multiplication.
    a. Thing
    b. Number system0
    c. Undefined
    d. Undefined

62. A _____ is 360° or 2∂ radians.
    a. Thing
    b. Turn0
    c. Undefined
    d. Undefined

63. _____ is a mathematical subject that includes the study of limits, derivatives, integrals, and power series and constitutes a major part of modern university curriculum.

a. Calculus0
b. Thing
c. Undefined
d. Undefined

64. In mathematics, a set is called _____ if there is a bijection between the set and some set of the form {1, 2, ..., n} where n is a natural number.
   a. Thing
   b. Finite0
   c. Undefined
   d. Undefined

65. In mathematics, an _____ number is any real number that is not a rational number- that is, it is a number which cannot be expressed as a fraction m/n, where m and n are integers.
   a. Thing
   b. Irrational0
   c. Undefined
   d. Undefined

66. In mathematics, an _____ is any real number that is not a rational number ¡ª that is, it is a number which cannot be expressed as m/n, where m and n are integers.
   a. Thing
   b. Irrational number0
   c. Undefined
   d. Undefined

67. Leonhard _____ was a pioneering Swiss mathematician and physicist, who spent most of his life in Russia and Germany.
   a. Person
   b. Euler0
   c. Undefined
   d. Undefined

68. _____ was a pioneering Swiss mathematician and physicist, who spent most of his life in Russia and Germany.
   a. Person
   b. Leonhard Euler0
   c. Undefined
   d. Undefined

69. In mathematics, _____ occurs when the growth rate of a function is always proportional to the function's current size.
   a. Exponential growth0
   b. Thing
   c. Undefined
   d. Undefined

70. _____ is a decrease that follows an exponential function.
   a. Exponential decay0
   b. Thing
   c. Undefined
   d. Undefined

71. _____ interest refers to the fact that whenever interest is calculated, it is based not only on the original principal, but also on any unpaid interest that has been added to the principal.
   a. Thing
   b. Compound0
   c. Undefined
   d. Undefined

72. _____ refers to the fact that whenever interest is calculated, it is based not only on the original principal, but also on any unpaid interest that has been added to the principal. The more frequently interest is compounded, the faster the balance grows.

Chapter 2. Additional Elementary Functions

a. Concept
b. Compound interest0
c. Undefined
d. Undefined

73. _____ is a way of expressing a number as a fraction of 100 per cent meaning "per hundred".
a. Thing
b. Percent0
c. Undefined
d. Undefined

74. In business, particularly accounting, a _____ is the time intervals that the accounts, statement, payments, or other calculations cover.
a. Thing
b. Period0
c. Undefined
d. Undefined

75. An _____ is the fee paid on borrow money.
a. Interest rate0
b. Concept
c. Undefined
d. Undefined

76. _____ is a kind of property which exists as magnitude or multitude. It is among the basic classes of things along with quality, substance, change, and relation.
a. Thing
b. Amount0
c. Undefined
d. Undefined

77. In elementary algebra, an _____ is a set that contains every real number between two indicated numbers and may contain the two numbers themselves.
a. Thing
b. Interval0
c. Undefined
d. Undefined

78. In mathematics, a _____ in elementary terms is any of a variety of different functions from geometry, such as rotations, reflections and translations.
a. Thing
b. Transformation0
c. Undefined
d. Undefined

79. A _____ is a negotiable instrument instructing a financial institution to pay a specific amount of a specific currency from a specific demand account held in the maker/depositor's name with that institution. Both the maker and payee may be natural persons or legal entities.
a. Check0
b. Thing
c. Undefined
d. Undefined

80. An _____ is a combination of numbers, operators, grouping symbols and/or free variables and bound variables arranged in a meaningful way which can be evaluated..
a. Thing
b. Expression0
c. Undefined
d. Undefined

81. _____ studies and addresses the ways in which individuals, businesses, and organizations raise, allocate, and use monetary resources over time, taking into account the risks entailed in their projects

Chapter 2. Additional Elementary Functions

    a. Thing
    c. Undefined
    b. Finance0
    d. Undefined

82. _____ usually refers to money in the form of liquid currency, such as banknotes or coins.
    a. Cash0
    b. Thing
    c. Undefined
    d. Undefined

83. In Graph theory, a _____ is a digraph with weighted edges.
    a. Concept
    b. Network0
    c. Undefined
    d. Undefined

84. In mathematics, a _____ is the result of multiplying, or an expression that identifies factors to be multiplied.
    a. Product0
    b. Thing
    c. Undefined
    d. Undefined

85. The _____ refers to a relationship between the duration of learning or experience and the resulting progress
    a. Learning curve0
    b. Thing
    c. Undefined
    d. Undefined

86. _____ are activities that are governed by a set of rules or customs and often engaged in competitively.
    a. Sports0
    b. Thing
    c. Undefined
    d. Undefined

87. A _____ is a form of periodic payment from an employer to an employee, which is specified in an employment contract.
    a. Salary0
    b. Thing
    c. Undefined
    d. Undefined

88. _____ is electromagnetic radiation with a wavelength that is visible to the eye (visible _____) or, in a technical or scientific context, electromagnetic radiation of any wavelength.
    a. Light0
    b. Thing
    c. Undefined
    d. Undefined

89. In epidemiology, an _____ is a disease that appears as new cases in a given human population, during a given period, at a rate that substantially exceeds with is "expected," based on recent experience.
    a. Thing
    b. Epidemic0
    c. Undefined
    d. Undefined

90. The _____ is the total number of human beings alive on the planet Earth at a given time.
    a. World population0
    b. Thing
    c. Undefined
    d. Undefined

91. In sociology and biology a _____ is the collection of people or organisms of a particular species living in a given geographic area or space, usually measured by a census.

Chapter 2. Additional Elementary Functions

    a. Thing
    b. Population0
    c. Undefined
    d. Undefined

92. _____ is change in population over time, and can be quantified as the change in the number of individuals in a population per unit time.
    a. Thing
    b. Population growth0
    c. Undefined
    d. Undefined

93. _____ is a statistical measure of the average length of survival of a living thing.
    a. Life expectancy0
    b. Thing
    c. Undefined
    d. Undefined

94. _____ element of an element x with respect to a binary operation * with identity element e is an element y such that x * y = y * x = e. In particular,
    a. Thing
    b. Inverse0
    c. Undefined
    d. Undefined

95. An _____ is a function which does the reverse of a given function.
    a. Inverse function0
    b. Thing
    c. Undefined
    d. Undefined

96. A _____ is a function for which, intuitively, small changes in the input result in small changes in the output.
    a. Continuous function0
    b. Event
    c. Undefined
    d. Undefined

97. An _____ is a collection of two not necessarily distinct objects, one of which is distinguished as the first coordinate and the other as the second coordinate.
    a. Thing
    b. Ordered pair0
    c. Undefined
    d. Undefined

98. _____ means "constancy", i.e. if something retains a certain feature even after we change a way of looking at it, then it is symmetric.
    a. Symmetry0
    b. Thing
    c. Undefined
    d. Undefined

99. In mathematics, the conjugate _____ or adjoint matrix of an m-by-n matrix A with complex entries is the n-by-m matrix A* obtained from A by taking the transpose and then taking the complex conjugate of each entry.
    a. Pairs0
    b. Thing
    c. Undefined
    d. Undefined

100. In mathematics, a _____ of a number x is the exponent y of the power by such that $x = b^y$. The value used for the base b must be neither 0 nor 1, nor a root of 1 in the case of the extension to complex numbers, and is typically 10, e, or 2.
    a. Thing
    b. Logarithm0
    c. Undefined
    d. Undefined

101. Equivalence is the condition of being _____ or essentially equal.

Chapter 2. Additional Elementary Functions

a. Equivalent0
b. Thing
c. Undefined
d. Undefined

102. In mathematics, a _____ is a demonstration that, assuming certain axioms, some statement is necessarily true.
a. Proof0
b. Thing
c. Undefined
d. Undefined

103. In mathematics, _____ is the decomposition of an object into a product of other objects, or factors, which when multiplied together give the original.
a. Factoring0
b. Thing
c. Undefined
d. Undefined

104. _____ is the logarithm to the base e, where e is an irrational constant approximately equal to 2.718281828459.
a. Natural logarithm0
b. Thing
c. Undefined
d. Undefined

105. In mathematics, the _____ is the logarithm with base 10.
a. Common logarithm0
b. Thing
c. Undefined
d. Undefined

106. In mathematics, a _____ is a number in the form of a + bi where a and b are real numbers, and i is the imaginary unit, with the property i 2 = −1. The real number a is called the real part of the _____, and the real number b is the imaginary part.
a. Complex number0
b. Thing
c. Undefined
d. Undefined

107. In mathematics, the _____ of two sets A and B is the set that contains all elements of A that also belong to B (or equivalently, all elements of B that also belong to A), but no other elements.
a. Intersection0
b. Thing
c. Undefined
d. Undefined

108. _____ or investing is a term with several closely-related meanings in business management, finance and economics, related to saving or deferring consumption.
a. Investment0
b. Thing
c. Undefined
d. Undefined

109. The _____ is the period of time required for a quantity to double in size or value.
a. Thing
b. Doubling time0
c. Undefined
d. Undefined

110. The _____, the average in everyday English, which is also called the arithmetic _____ (and is distinguished from the geometric _____ or harmonic _____). The average is also called the sample _____. The expected value of a random variable, which is also called the population _____.

Chapter 2. Additional Elementary Functions

a. Mean0
b. Thing
c. Undefined
d. Undefined

111. In finance and economics, _____ is the process of finding the present value of an amount of cash at some future date, and along with compounding cash forms the basis of time value of money calculations.
    a. Discount0
    b. Thing
    c. Undefined
    d. Undefined

112. The _____, i.e., acoustic intensity is defined as the sound power P_{ac} per unit area A.
    a. Sound intensity0
    b. Thing
    c. Undefined
    d. Undefined

113. A _____ is a function that assigns a number to subsets of a given set.
    a. Measure0
    b. Thing
    c. Undefined
    d. Undefined

114. In Euclidean geometry, a uniform _____ is a linear transformation that enlargers or diminishes objects, and whose _____ factor is the same in all directions. This is also called homothethy.
    a. Thing
    b. Scale0
    c. Undefined
    d. Undefined

115. The _____ relative to a specified or implied reference level.
    a. Thing
    b. Decibel0
    c. Undefined
    d. Undefined

116. In plane geometry, a _____ is a polygon with four equal sides, four right angles, and parallel opposite sides. In algebra, the _____ of a number is that number multiplied by itself.
    a. Square0
    b. Thing
    c. Undefined
    d. Undefined

117. _____ is the production of food, feed, fiber, fuel and other goods by the systematic raizing of plants and animals.
    a. Agriculture0
    b. Thing
    c. Undefined
    d. Undefined

118. _____ of a single or multiple future payments is the nominal amounts of money to change hands at some future date, discounted to account for the time value of money, and other factors such as investment risk.
    a. Thing
    b. Present value0
    c. Undefined
    d. Undefined

119. _____ measures the nominal future sum of money that a given sum of money is "worth" at a specified time in the future assuming a certain interest rate; this value does not include corrections for inflation or other factors that affect the true value of money in the future.
    a. Thing
    b. Future value0
    c. Undefined
    d. Undefined

Chapter 2. Additional Elementary Functions

120. A _____ or CD is a time deposit, a financial product commonly offered to consumers by banks, thrift institutions, and credit unions.
   a. Certificate of deposit0
   b. Thing
   c. Undefined
   d. Undefined

121. In economics, supply and _____ describe market relations between prospective sellers and buyers of a good.
   a. Thing
   b. Demand0
   c. Undefined
   d. Undefined

122. _____ is the estimation of a physical quantity such as distance, energy, temperature, or time.
   a. Measurement0
   b. Thing
   c. Undefined
   d. Undefined

123. In mathematics and its applications, a _____ is a system for assigning an n-tuple of numbers or scalars to each point in an n-dimensional space.
   a. Concept
   b. Coordinate system0
   c. Undefined
   d. Undefined

124. A _____ is the result of the addition of a set of numbers. The numbers may be natural numbers, complex numbers, matrices, or still more complicated objects. An infinite _____ is a subtle procedure known as a series.
   a. Thing
   b. Sum0
   c. Undefined
   d. Undefined

125. In mathematics, a _____ set is the complement of a meager set. A meager set is one which is the countable union of nowhere dense sets.
   a. Thing
   b. Residual0
   c. Undefined
   d. Undefined

126. In common philosophical language, a proposition or _____, is the content of an assertion, that is, it is true-or-false and defined by the meaning of a particular piece of language.
   a. Concept
   b. Statement0
   c. Undefined
   d. Undefined

Chapter 3. The Derivative

1. A _____ is a symbolic representation denoting a quantity or expression. It often represents an "unknown" quantity that has the potential to change.
   - a. Thing
   - b. Variable0
   - c. Undefined
   - d. Undefined

2. _____ is a branch of mathematics concerning the study of structure, relation and quantity.
   - a. Concept
   - b. Algebra0
   - c. Undefined
   - d. Undefined

3. _____ is a mathematical subject that includes the study of limits, derivatives, integrals, and power series and constitutes a major part of modern university curriculum.
   - a. Thing
   - b. Calculus0
   - c. Undefined
   - d. Undefined

4. Sir Isaac _____, was an English physicist, mathematician, astronomer, natural philosopher, and alchemist, regarded by many as the greatest figure in the history of science
   - a. Newton0
   - b. Person
   - c. Undefined
   - d. Undefined

5. _____ was a German polymath who wrote mostly in Latin and French.
   - a. Thing
   - b. Gottfried Wilhelm von Leibniz0
   - c. Undefined
   - d. Undefined

6. _____ was a German mathematician and philosopher. He invented calculus independently of Newton, and his notation is the one in general use since.
   - a. Leibniz0
   - b. Person
   - c. Undefined
   - d. Undefined

7. Sir _____ was an English physicist, mathematician, astronomer, natural philosopher, and alchemist, regarded by many as the greatest figure in the history of science.
   - a. Isaac Newton0
   - b. Person
   - c. Undefined
   - d. Undefined

8. In mathematics, an _____, mean, or central tendency of a data set refers to a measure of the "middle" or "expected" value of the data set.
   - a. Concept
   - b. Average0
   - c. Undefined
   - d. Undefined

9. _____ is a business term for the amount of money that a company receives from its activities in a given period, mostly from sales of products and/or services to customers
   - a. Thing
   - b. Revenue0
   - c. Undefined
   - d. Undefined

10. A _____ is a special kind of ratio, indicating a relationship between two measurements with different units, such as miles to gallons or cents to pounds.

a. Thing
b. Rate0
c. Undefined
d. Undefined

11. A _____ is a quantity that denotes the proportional amount or magnitude of one quantity relative to another.
   a. Thing
   b. Ratio0
   c. Undefined
   d. Undefined

12. The mathematical concept of a _____ expresses the intuitive idea of deterministic dependence between two quantities, one of which is viewed as primary and the other as secondary. A _____ then is a way to associate a unique output for each input of a specified type, for example, a real number or an element of a given set.
   a. Function0
   b. Thing
   c. Undefined
   d. Undefined

13. In mathematics, a _____ is the end result of a division problem. It can also be expressed as the number of times the divisor divides into the dividend.
   a. Thing
   b. Quotient0
   c. Undefined
   d. Undefined

14. An _____ is a combination of numbers, operators, grouping symbols and/or free variables and bound variables arranged in a meaningful way which can be evaluated..
   a. Expression0
   b. Thing
   c. Undefined
   d. Undefined

15. The function difference divided by the point difference is known as the _____
   a. Difference quotient0
   b. Thing
   c. Undefined
   d. Undefined

16. _____ of an object is its speed in a particular direction.
   a. Velocity0
   b. Thing
   c. Undefined
   d. Undefined

17. A _____ is a set of numbers that designate location in a given reference system, such as x,y in a planar _____ system or an x,y,z in a three-dimensional _____ system.
   a. Coordinate0
   b. Thing
   c. Undefined
   d. Undefined

18. _____, Greek for "knowledge of nature," is the branch of science concerned with the discovery and characterization of universal laws which govern matter, energy, space, and time.
   a. Physics0
   b. Thing
   c. Undefined
   d. Undefined

19. In elementary algebra, an _____ is a set that contains every real number between two indicated numbers and may contain the two numbers themselves.
   a. Interval0
   b. Thing
   c. Undefined
   d. Undefined

Chapter 3. The Derivative

20. In mathematics, an _____ is any of the arguments, i.e. "inputs", to a function. Thus if we have a function f(x), then x is a _____.
   a. Independent variable0
   b. Thing
   c. Undefined
   d. Undefined

21. In a function the _____, is the variable which is the value, i.e. the "output", of the function.
   a. Thing
   b. Dependent variable0
   c. Undefined
   d. Undefined

22. _____ is often used to describe the measurement of the steepness, incline, gradient, or grade of a straight line. The _____ is defined as the ratio of the "rise" divided by the "run" between two points on a line, or in other words, the ratio of the altitude change to the horizontal distance between any two points on the line.
   a. Thing
   b. Slope0
   c. Undefined
   d. Undefined

23. In mathematics, the _____ f is the collection of all ordered pairs . In particular, graph means the graphical representation of this collection, in the form of a curve or surface, together with axes, etc. Graphing on a Cartesian plane is sometimes referred to as curve sketching.
   a. Graph of a function0
   b. Thing
   c. Undefined
   d. Undefined

24. _____ is a trigonometric function that is the reciprocal of cosine.
   a. Thing
   b. Secant0
   c. Undefined
   d. Undefined

25. _____ of a curve is a line that intersects two or more points on the curve.
   a. Secant line0
   b. Thing
   c. Undefined
   d. Undefined

26. In trigonometry, the _____ is a function defined as tan x = $^{\sin x}/_{\cos x}$. The function is so-named because it can be defined as the length of a certain segment of a _____ (in the geometric sense) to the unit circle. In plane geometry, a line is _____ to a curve, at some point, if both line and curve pass through the point with the same direction.
   a. Tangent0
   b. Thing
   c. Undefined
   d. Undefined

27. In Euclidean geometry, a _____ is the set of all points in a plane at a fixed distance, called the radius, from a given point, the center.
   a. Circle0
   b. Thing
   c. Undefined
   d. Undefined

28. _____ has two distinct but etymologically-related meanings: one in geometry and one in trigonometry.
   a. Tangent line0
   b. Thing
   c. Undefined
   d. Undefined

29. In mathematics, a _____ is a two-dimensional manifold or surface that is perfectly flat.

a. Plane0
b. Thing
c. Undefined
d. Undefined

30. _____ are the basic objects of study in graph theory. Informally speaking, a graph is a set of objects called points, nodes, or vertices connected by links called lines or edges.
    a. Graphs0
    b. Thing
    c. Undefined
    d. Undefined

31. The act of _____ is the calculated approximation of a result which is usable even if input data may be incomplete, uncertain, or noisy.
    a. Thing
    b. Estimating0
    c. Undefined
    d. Undefined

32. An _____ is a straight line around which a geometric figure can be rotated.
    a. Thing
    b. Axis0
    c. Undefined
    d. Undefined

33. In astronomy, geography, geometry and related sciences and contexts, a plane is said to be _____ at a given point if it is locally perpendicular to the gradient of the gravity field, i.e., with the direction of the gravitational force at that point.
    a. Horizontal0
    b. Thing
    c. Undefined
    d. Undefined

34. A _____ is a numeral used to indicate a count. The most common use of the word today is to name the part of a fraction that tells the number or count of equal parts.
    a. Numerator0
    b. Thing
    c. Undefined
    d. Undefined

35. A _____ is the part of a fraction that tells how many equal parts make up a whole, and which is used in the name of the fraction: "halves", "thirds", "fourths" or "quarters", "fifths" and so on.
    a. Denominator0
    b. Concept
    c. Undefined
    d. Undefined

36. In physics, _____ is an influence that may cause an object to accelerate. It may be experienced as a lift, a push, or a pull. The actual acceleration of the body is determined by the vector sum of all forces acting on it, known as net _____ or resultant _____.
    a. Force0
    b. Thing
    c. Undefined
    d. Undefined

37. A _____ is the quantity that defines certain relatively constant characteristics of systems or functions..
    a. Thing
    b. Parameter0
    c. Undefined
    d. Undefined

38. _____ is the state of being greater than any finite real or natural number, however large.
    a. Infinite0
    b. Thing
    c. Undefined
    d. Undefined

Chapter 3. The Derivative

39. In set theory, an _____ is a set that is not a finite set. Infinite sets may be countable or uncountable.
   a. Infinite set0
   b. Thing
   c. Undefined
   d. Undefined

40. In mathematics, a set is called _____ if there is a bijection between the set and some set of the form {1, 2, ..., n} where n is a natural number.
   a. Finite0
   b. Thing
   c. Undefined
   d. Undefined

41. In mathematics, a _____ occurs if there is a bijection between the set and some set of the form 1, 2, ..., n where n is a natural number.
   a. Finite set0
   b. Concept
   c. Undefined
   d. Undefined

42. _____ is the middle point of a line segment.
   a. Thing
   b. Midpoint0
   c. Undefined
   d. Undefined

43. In mathematics, a _____ may be described informally as a number that can be given by an infinite decimal representation.
   a. Real number0
   b. Thing
   c. Undefined
   d. Undefined

44. In mathematics, the term _____ is applied to certain functions. There are two common ways it is applied: these are related historically, but diverged somewhat during the twentieth century.
   a. Functional0
   b. Thing
   c. Undefined
   d. Undefined

45. A _____ is 360° or 2ð radians.
   a. Turn0
   b. Thing
   c. Undefined
   d. Undefined

46. In mathematics, a _____ is a statement that can be proved on the basis of explicitly stated or previously agreed assumptions.
   a. Theorem0
   b. Thing
   c. Undefined
   d. Undefined

47. In mathematics, a _____ is an expression that is constructed from one or more variables and constants, using only the operations of addition, subtraction, multiplication, and constant positive whole number exponents. is a _____. Note in particular that division by an expression containing a variable is not in general allowed in polynomials. [1]
   a. Thing
   b. Polynomial0
   c. Undefined
   d. Undefined

48. In calculus and other branches of mathematical analysis, an _____ is an algebraic expression obtained in the context of limits.

a. Thing
b. Indeterminate form0
c. Undefined
d. Undefined

49. _____ is the transport of people on a trip/journey or the process or time involved in a person or object moving from one location to another.
a. Travel0
b. Thing
c. Undefined
d. Undefined

50. There are two simple _____ the greatest common factor and least common multiple: standard factorization and prime factorization.
a. Thing
b. Methods for finding0
c. Undefined
d. Undefined

51. An _____ of a product of sums expresses it as a sum of products by using the fact that multiplication distributes over addition.
a. Thing
b. Expansion0
c. Undefined
d. Undefined

52. When _____ symmetry one can determine whether or not an object is symmetric with respect to a given mathematical operation, if, when applied to the object, this operation does not change the object or its appearance.
a. Investigating0
b. Thing
c. Undefined
d. Undefined

53. The _____ are the only integral domain whose positive elements are well-ordered, and in which order is preserved by addition. Like the natural numbers, the _____ form a countably infinite set. The set of all _____ is usually denoted in mathematics by a boldface Z .
a. Thing
b. Integers0
c. Undefined
d. Undefined

54. In linear algebra, the _____ of an n-by-n square matrix A is defined to be the sum of the elements on the main diagonal of A,
a. Trace0
b. Thing
c. Undefined
d. Undefined

55. A _____ is an individual or household that purchases and uses goods and services generated within the economy.
a. Thing
b. Consumer0
c. Undefined
d. Undefined

56. _____, from Latin meaning "to make progress", is defined in two different ways. Pure economic _____ is the increase in wealth that an investor has from making an investment, taking into consideration all costs associated with that investment including the opportunity cost of capital.
a. Profit0
b. Thing
c. Undefined
d. Undefined

Chapter 3. The Derivative

57. In set theory and other branches of mathematics, the _____ of a collection of sets is the set that contains everything that belongs to any of the sets, but nothing else.
   a. Union0
   b. Thing
   c. Undefined
   d. Undefined

58. In geometry, an _____ of a triangle is a straight line through a vertex and perpendicular to (i.e. forming a right angle with) the opposite side or an extension of the opposite side.
   a. Altitude0
   b. Concept
   c. Undefined
   d. Undefined

59. A _____ is a function that assigns a number to subsets of a given set.
   a. Thing
   b. Measure0
   c. Undefined
   d. Undefined

60. _____ is a kind of property which exists as magnitude or multitude. It is among the basic classes of things along with quality, substance, change, and relation.
   a. Thing
   b. Amount0
   c. Undefined
   d. Undefined

61. In sociology and biology a _____ is the collection of people or organisms of a particular species living in a given geographic area or space, usually measured by a census.
   a. Population0
   b. Thing
   c. Undefined
   d. Undefined

62. The _____ is a measurement of how a function changes when the values of its inputs change.
   a. Thing
   b. Derivative0
   c. Undefined
   d. Undefined

63. _____, a field in mathematics, is the study of how functions change when their inputs change. The primary object of study in _____ is the derivative.
   a. Thing
   b. Differential calculus0
   c. Undefined
   d. Undefined

64. In mathematics, a _____ of a k-place relation $L \subseteq X_1 \times ... \times X_k$ is one of the sets X_j, $1 \leq j \leq k$. In the special case where k = 2 and $L \subseteq X_1 \times X_2$ is a function $L : X_1 \rightarrow X_2$, it is conventional to refer to X_1 as the _____ of the function and to refer to X_2 as the codomain of the function.
   a. Domain0
   b. Thing
   c. Undefined
   d. Undefined

65. An _____ is when two lines intersect somewhere on a plane creating a right angle at intersection
   a. Axes0
   b. Thing
   c. Undefined
   d. Undefined

66. _____ is a technique of numerical analysis to produce an estimate of the derivative of a mathematical function or function subroutine using values from the function and perhaps other knowledge about the function.

a. Numerical differentiation0 b. Thing
c. Undefined d. Undefined

67. A _____ is a set whose members are members of another set or a set contained within another set.
a. Subset0 b. Thing
c. Undefined d. Undefined

68. A _____ is a negotiable instrument instructing a financial institution to pay a specific amount of a specific currency from a specific demand account held in the maker/depositor's name with that institution. Both the maker and payee may be natural persons or legal entities.
a. Check0 b. Thing
c. Undefined d. Undefined

69. In mathematics and the mathematical sciences, a _____ is a fixed, but possibly unspecified, value. This is in contrast to a variable, which is not fixed.
a. Constant0 b. Thing
c. Undefined d. Undefined

70. _____ is a function whose values do not vary and thus are constant.
a. Thing b. Constant function0
c. Undefined d. Undefined

71. A _____ function is a function for which, intuitively, small changes in the input result in small changes in the output.
a. Event b. Continuous0
c. Undefined d. Undefined

72. _____ Any process by which a specified characteristic usually amplitude of the output of a device is prevented from exceeding a predetermined value.
a. Thing b. Limiting0
c. Undefined d. Undefined

73. In mathematics, a _____ is a countable collection of open covers of a topological space that satisfies certain separation axioms.
a. Thing b. Development0
c. Undefined d. Undefined

74. In common philosophical language, a proposition or _____, is the content of an assertion, that is, it is true-or-false and defined by the meaning of a particular piece of language.
a. Concept b. Statement0
c. Undefined d. Undefined

75. _____ is the fee paid on borrowed money.
a. Interest0 b. Thing
c. Undefined d. Undefined

Chapter 3. The Derivative

76. _____ interest refers to the fact that whenever interest is calculated, it is based not only on the original principal, but also on any unpaid interest that has been added to the principal.
   a. Thing
   b. Compound0
   c. Undefined
   d. Undefined

77. _____ refers to the fact that whenever interest is calculated, it is based not only on the original principal, but also on any unpaid interest that has been added to the principal. The more frequently interest is compounded, the faster the balance grows.
   a. Compound interest0
   b. Concept
   c. Undefined
   d. Undefined

78. _____ or investing is a term with several closely-related meanings in business management, finance and economics, related to saving or deferring consumption.
   a. Investment0
   b. Thing
   c. Undefined
   d. Undefined

79. In business, particularly accounting, a _____ is the time intervals that the accounts, statement, payments, or other calculations cover.
   a. Thing
   b. Period0
   c. Undefined
   d. Undefined

80. _____ is a synonym for information.
   a. Data0
   b. Thing
   c. Undefined
   d. Undefined

81. _____ is a temperature scale named after the German physicist Daniel Gabriel _____ , who proposed it in 1724.
   a. Thing
   b. Fahrenheit0
   c. Undefined
   d. Undefined

82. In mathematics, there are several meanings of _____ depending on the subject.
   a. Thing
   b. Degree0
   c. Undefined
   d. Undefined

83. _____ is a physical property of a system that underlies the common notions of hot and cold; something that is hotter has the greater _____ .
   a. Thing
   b. Temperature0
   c. Undefined
   d. Undefined

84. A _____ is the result of the addition of a set of numbers. The numbers may be natural numbers, complex numbers, matrices, or still more complicated objects. An infinite _____ is a subtle procedure known as a series.
   a. Thing
   b. Sum0
   c. Undefined
   d. Undefined

85. _____ has many meanings, most of which simply .

a. Power0
c. Undefined

b. Thing
d. Undefined

86. _____ are objects, characters, or other concrete representations of ideas, concepts, or other abstractions.
   a. Thing
   b. Symbols0
   c. Undefined
   d. Undefined

87. In mathematics, a _____ is a constant multiplicative factor of a certain object. The object can be such things as a variable, a vector, a function, etc. For example, the _____ of $9x^2$ is 9.
   a. Coefficient0
   b. Thing
   c. Undefined
   d. Undefined

88. _____ is a method for differentiating expressions involving exponentiation the power operation.
   a. Power rule0
   b. Thing
   c. Undefined
   d. Undefined

89. _____ is the change in total cost that arises when the quantity produced changes by one unit.
   a. Marginal cost0
   b. Thing
   c. Undefined
   d. Undefined

90. In mathematics, the _____ is a conic section generated by the intersection of a right circular conical surface and a plane parallel to a generating straight line of that surface. It can also be defined as locus of points in a plane which are equidistant from a given point.
   a. Thing
   b. Parabola0
   c. Undefined
   d. Undefined

91. In geometry, a _____ is a special kind of point, usually a corner of a polygon, polyhedron, or higher dimensional polytope. In the geometry of curves a _____ is a point of where the first derivative of curvature is zero. In graph theory, a _____ is the fundamental unit out of which graphs are formed
   a. Thing
   b. Vertex0
   c. Undefined
   d. Undefined

92. A _____ is a unit of length, usually used to measure distance, in a number of different systems, including Imperial units, United States customary units and Norwegian/Swedish mil. Its size can vary from system to system, but in each is between 1 and 10 kilometers. In contemporary English contexts _____ refers to either:
   a. Mile0
   b. Thing
   c. Undefined
   d. Undefined

93. In mathematics, a _____ is the result of multiplying, or an expression that identifies factors to be multiplied.
   a. Product0
   b. Thing
   c. Undefined
   d. Undefined

94. The _____ is a method of finding the derivative of a function that is the quotient of two other functions for which derivatives exist.

Chapter 3. The Derivative

    a. Quotient rule0   b. Thing
    c. Undefined   d. Undefined

95. In mathematics, _____ is an elementary arithmetic operation. When one of the numbers is a whole number, _____ is the repeated sum of the other number.
    a. Thing   b. Multiplication0
    c. Undefined   d. Undefined

96. The _____ governs the differentiation of products of differentiable functions.
    a. Product rule0   b. Thing
    c. Undefined   d. Undefined

97. In mathematics, _____ expressions is used to reduce the expression into the lowest possible term.
    a. Simplifying0   b. Thing
    c. Undefined   d. Undefined

98. _____ are procedures that allow people to exchange information by one of several methods.
    a. Communications0   b. Thing
    c. Undefined   d. Undefined

99. In economics, supply and _____ describe market relations between prospective sellers and buyers of a good.
    a. Thing   b. Demand0
    c. Undefined   d. Undefined

100. _____ was a U.S. pioneer in the fields of psychometrics and psychophysics. He conceived the approach to measurement known as the law of comparative judgment, and is well known for his contributions to factor analysis.
    a. Thurstone0   b. Person
    c. Undefined   d. Undefined

101. In calculus, the _____ is a formula for the derivative of the composite of two functions.
    a. Chain rule0   b. Concept
    c. Undefined   d. Undefined

102. _____ is a mathematical operation, written a^n, involving two numbers, the base a and the exponent n.
    a. Thing   b. Exponentiating0
    c. Undefined   d. Undefined

103. _____ is a mathematical operation, written a^n, involving two numbers, the base a and the exponent n.
    a. Thing   b. Exponentiation0
    c. Undefined   d. Undefined

104. In statistics, a _____ measure is one which is measuring what is supposed to measure.
    a. Valid0   b. Thing
    c. Undefined   d. Undefined

105. An _____ is the fee paid on borrow money.

Chapter 3. The Derivative

a. Concept
c. Undefined
b. Interest rate0
d. Undefined

106. _____ is the level of functional and/or metabolic efficiency of an organism at both the micro level.
a. Health0
b. Thing
c. Undefined
d. Undefined

107. _____ is the use of marginal concepts within economics. Marginal concepts include marginal cost, marginal productivity and marginal utility, the law of diminishing rates of substitution, and the law of diminishing marginal utility.
a. Marginal analysis0
b. Thing
c. Undefined
d. Undefined

108. _____ is the extra revenue that an additional unit of product will bring a firm. It can also be described as the change in total revenue/change in number of units sold.
a. Marginal revenue0
b. Thing
c. Undefined
d. Undefined

109. A _____ is a deliberate process for transforming one or more inputs into one or more results.
a. Thing
b. Calculation0
c. Undefined
d. Undefined

110. In mathematics and its applications, a _____ is a system for assigning an n-tuple of numbers or scalars to each point in an n-dimensional space.
a. Coordinate system0
b. Concept
c. Undefined
d. Undefined

111. In mathematics, the _____ of two sets A and B is the set that contains all elements of A that also belong to B (or equivalently, all elements of B that also belong to A), but no other elements.
a. Intersection0
b. Thing
c. Undefined
d. Undefined

112. Any point where a graph makes contact with an coordinate axis is called an _____ of the graph
a. Thing
b. Intercept0
c. Undefined
d. Undefined

113. The _____, the average in everyday English, which is also called the arithmetic _____ (and is distinguished from the geometric _____ or harmonic _____). The average is also called the sample _____. The expected value of a random variable, which is also called the population _____.
a. Thing
b. Mean0
c. Undefined
d. Undefined

114. _____ is the application of tools and a processing medium to the transformation of raw materials into finished goods for sale.
a. Thing
b. Manufacturing0
c. Undefined
d. Undefined

Chapter 3. The Derivative

115. The _____ of measurement are a globally standardized and modernized form of the metric system.
    a. Thing
    b. Units0
    c. Undefined
    d. Undefined

116. The word _____ comes from the Latin word linearis, which means created by lines.
    a. Thing
    b. Linear0
    c. Undefined
    d. Undefined

117. Fixed costs are expenses whose total does not change in proportion to the activity of a business.Unit fixed costs decline with volume following a retangular hyperbola as the volume of production.Variable costs by contrast change in relation to the activity of a business such as sales or production volume.Along with variable costs,fixed costs make up one of the two components of total cost. In the most simple production function total cost is equal to fixed costs plus variable costs.In accounting terminology, fixed costs will broadly include all costs which are not included in cost of goods sold, and variable costs are those captured in costs of goods sold. The implicit assumption required to make the equivalence between the accounting and economics terminology is that the accounting period is equal to the period in which fixed costs do not vary in relation to production. In practice, this equivalence does not always hold and depending on the period under consideration by management, some overhead expenses can be adjusted by management, and the specific allocation of each expense to each category will be decided under cost accounting.In business planning and management accounting, usage of the terms fixed costs, variable costs and others will often differ from usage in economics, and may depend on the intended use. For example, costs may be segregated into per unit costs fixed costs per period, and variable costs as a proportion of revenue. Capital expenditures will usually be allocated separately, and depending on the purpose, a portion may be regularly allocated to expenses as depreciation and amortization and seen as a _____ per period, or the entire amount may be considered upfront fixed costs.
    a. Thing
    b. Fixed cost0
    c. Undefined
    d. Undefined

118. _____ are expenses whose total does not change in proportion to the activity of a business, within the relevant time period or scale of production
    a. Thing
    b. Fixed costs0
    c. Undefined
    d. Undefined

119. _____ is a regression method that models the relationship between a dependent variable Y, independent variables Xp, and a random term à.
    a. Thing
    b. Linear regression0
    c. Undefined
    d. Undefined

120. In mathematics, the _____ of a function is the set of all "output" values produced by that function. Given a function $f : A \to B$, the _____ of f, is defined to be the set $\{x \in B : x = f(a) \text{ for some } a \in A\}$.
    a. Range0
    b. Thing
    c. Undefined
    d. Undefined

121. In mathematics, the _____ (or modulus) of a real number is its numerical value without regard to its sign.
    a. Thing
    b. Absolute value0
    c. Undefined
    d. Undefined

122. Mathematical _____ is used to represent ideas.

Chapter 3. The Derivative

a. Thing
b. Notation0
c. Undefined
d. Undefined

123. In a mathematical proof or a syllogism, a _____ is a statement that is the logical consequence of preceding statements.
   a. Conclusion0
   b. Concept
   c. Undefined
   d. Undefined

124. In mathematics, in the field of group theory, a _____ of a group is a quasisimple subnormal subgroup.
   a. Concept
   b. Component0
   c. Undefined
   d. Undefined

125. In geometry, the _____ of an object is a point in some sense in the middle of the object.
   a. Thing
   b. Center0
   c. Undefined
   d. Undefined

126. A _____ is a polynomial function of the form $f(x) = ax^2 + bx + c$, where a, b, c are real numbers and a , 0.
   a. Event
   b. Quadratic function0
   c. Undefined
   d. Undefined

127. _____ is a function of the form
   a. Cubic function0
   b. Thing
   c. Undefined
   d. Undefined

128. In geographic information systems, a _____ comprises an entity with a geographic location, typically determined by points, arcs, or polygons. Carriageways and cadastres exemplify _____ data.
   a. Feature0
   b. Thing
   c. Undefined
   d. Undefined

Chapter 4. Graphing and Optimization

1. _____, from Latin meaning "to make progress", is defined in two different ways. Pure economic _____ is the increase in wealth that an investor has from making an investment, taking into consideration all costs associated with that investment including the opportunity cost of capital.
   a. Profit0
   b. Thing
   c. Undefined
   d. Undefined

2. _____ are the basic objects of study in graph theory. Informally speaking, a graph is a set of objects called points, nodes, or vertices connected by links called lines or edges.
   a. Thing
   b. Graphs0
   c. Undefined
   d. Undefined

3. _____ are objects, characters, or other concrete representations of ideas, concepts, or other abstractions.
   a. Thing
   b. Symbols0
   c. Undefined
   d. Undefined

4. In mathematics, the concept of a _____ tries to capture the intuitive idea of a geometrical one-dimensional and continuous object. A simple example is the circle.
   a. Thing
   b. Curve0
   c. Undefined
   d. Undefined

5. Graphing on a Cartesian plane is sometimes referred to as _____.
   a. Curve sketching0
   b. Thing
   c. Undefined
   d. Undefined

6. _____ is a free computer algebra system based on a 1982 version of Macsyma
   a. Thing
   b. Maxima0
   c. Undefined
   d. Undefined

7. _____ are points in the domain of a function at which the function takes a largest value or smallest value, either within a given neighborhood or on the function domain in its entirety.
   a. Thing
   b. Maxima and minima0
   c. Undefined
   d. Undefined

8. _____ is a mathematical subject that includes the study of limits, derivatives, integrals, and power series and constitutes a major part of modern university curriculum.
   a. Thing
   b. Calculus0
   c. Undefined
   d. Undefined

9. The _____ is a measurement of how a function changes when the values of its inputs change.
   a. Derivative0
   b. Thing
   c. Undefined
   d. Undefined

10. In mathematics, a _____ is a countable collection of open covers of a topological space that satisfies certain separation axioms.
    a. Development0
    b. Thing
    c. Undefined
    d. Undefined

11. The mathematical concept of a _____ expresses the intuitive idea of deterministic dependence between two quantities, one of which is viewed as primary and the other as secondary. A _____ then is a way to associate a unique output for each input of a specified type, for example, a real number or an element of a given set.
   a. Function0
   b. Thing
   c. Undefined
   d. Undefined

12. In mathematics, maxima and _____, known collectively as extrema, are points in the domain of a function at which the function takes a largest value.
   a. Thing
   b. Minima0
   c. Undefined
   d. Undefined

13. Compass and straightedge or ruler-and-compass _____ is the _____ of lengths or angles using only an idealized ruler and compass.
   a. Thing
   b. Construction0
   c. Undefined
   d. Undefined

14. In mathematics, the _____ f is the collection of all ordered pairs. In particular, graph means the graphical representation of this collection, in the form of a curve or surface, together with axes, etc. Graphing on a Cartesian plane is sometimes referred to as curve sketching.
   a. Thing
   b. Graph of a function0
   c. Undefined
   d. Undefined

15. In computer science, an _____ is the problem of finding the best solution from all feasible solutions.
   a. Thing
   b. Optimization problem0
   c. Undefined
   d. Undefined

16. A _____ function is a function for which, intuitively, small changes in the input result in small changes in the output.
   a. Event
   b. Continuous0
   c. Undefined
   d. Undefined

17. In elementary algebra, an _____ is a set that contains every real number between two indicated numbers and may contain the two numbers themselves.
   a. Thing
   b. Interval0
   c. Undefined
   d. Undefined

18. Continuous functions are of utmost importance in mathematics and applications. However, not all functions are continuous. If a function is not continuous at a point in its domain, one says that it has a _____ there. The set of all points of _____ of a function may be a discrete set, a dense set, or even the entire domain of the function.
   a. Discontinuity0
   b. Thing
   c. Undefined
   d. Undefined

19. In business, particularly accounting, a _____ is the time intervals that the accounts, statement, payments, or other calculations cover.

Chapter 4. Graphing and Optimization 41

    a. Thing
    c. Undefined
    b. Period0
    d. Undefined

20. _____ is a physical property of a system that underlies the common notions of hot and cold; something that is hotter has the greater _____.
    a. Temperature0
    c. Undefined
    b. Thing
    d. Undefined

21. _____ is a list of goods and materials, or those goods and materials themselves, held available in stock by a business
    a. Inventory0
    c. Undefined
    b. Thing
    d. Undefined

22. In mathematics, _____ geometry was the traditional name for the geometry of three-dimensional Euclidean space — for practical purposes the kind of space we live in.
    a. Thing
    c. Undefined
    b. Solid0
    d. Undefined

23. In mathematics, a _____ is a statement that can be proved on the basis of explicitly stated or previously agreed assumptions.
    a. Theorem0
    c. Undefined
    b. Thing
    d. Undefined

24. In mathematics and the mathematical sciences, a _____ is a fixed, but possibly unspecified, value. This is in contrast to a variable, which is not fixed.
    a. Constant0
    c. Undefined
    b. Thing
    d. Undefined

25. _____ is a function whose values do not vary and thus are constant.
    a. Constant function0
    c. Undefined
    b. Thing
    d. Undefined

26. In mathematics, a _____ is an expression that is constructed from one or more variables and constants, using only the operations of addition, subtraction, multiplication, and constant positive whole number exponents. is a _____. Note in particular that division by an expression containing a variable is not in general allowed in polynomials. [1]
    a. Thing
    c. Undefined
    b. Polynomial0
    d. Undefined

27. In mathematics, an inequality is a statement about the relative size or order of two objects. For example 14 > 10, or 14 is _____ 10.
    a. Greater than0
    c. Undefined
    b. Thing
    d. Undefined

28. In mathematics, a _____ number is a number which can be expressed as a ratio of two integers. Non-integer _____ numbers (commonly called fractions) are usually written as the vulgar fraction a / b, where b is not zero.

a. Rational0
c. Undefined
b. Thing
d. Undefined

29. In mathematics, a _____ is any function which can be written as the ratio of two polynomial functions.
    a. Thing
    b. Rational function0
    c. Undefined
    d. Undefined

30. A _____ is the part of a fraction that tells how many equal parts make up a whole, and which is used in the name of the fraction: "halves", "thirds", "fourths" or "quarters", "fifths" and so on.
    a. Denominator0
    b. Concept
    c. Undefined
    d. Undefined

31. The _____ integers are all the integers from zero on upwards.
    a. Thing
    b. Nonnegative0
    c. Undefined
    d. Undefined

32. A _____ fraction is a fraction in which the absolute value of the numerator is less than the denominator--hence, the absolute value of the fraction is less than 1.
    a. Thing
    b. Proper0
    c. Undefined
    d. Undefined

33. _____ is the state of being greater than any finite real or natural number, however large.
    a. Thing
    b. Infinite0
    c. Undefined
    d. Undefined

34. A _____ is a number that is less than zero.
    a. Thing
    b. Negative number0
    c. Undefined
    d. Undefined

35. In common philosophical language, a proposition or _____, is the content of an assertion, that is, it is true-or-false and defined by the meaning of a particular piece of language.
    a. Statement0
    b. Concept
    c. Undefined
    d. Undefined

36. _____ is a straight line or curve A to which another curve B the one being studied approaches closer and closer as one moves along it.
    a. Vertical asymptote0
    b. Thing
    c. Undefined
    d. Undefined

37. An _____ is a straight line or curve A to which another curve B approaches closer and closer as one moves along it. As one moves along B, the space between it and the _____ A becomes smaller and smaller, and can in fact be made as small as one could wish by going far enough along. A curve may or may not touch or cross its _____. In fact, the curve may intersect the _____ an infinite number of times.
    a. Asymptote0
    b. Thing
    c. Undefined
    d. Undefined

Chapter 4. Graphing and Optimization

38. In mathematics, an _____ is a statement about the relative size or order of two objects.
    a. Thing
    b. Inequality0
    c. Undefined
    d. Undefined

39. Deductive _____ is the kind of _____ in which the conclusion is necessitated by, or reached from, previously known facts (the premises).
    a. Thing
    b. Reasoning0
    c. Undefined
    d. Undefined

40. An _____ is a straight line around which a geometric figure can be rotated.
    a. Axis0
    b. Thing
    c. Undefined
    d. Undefined

41. A _____ is a one-dimensional picture in which the integers are shown as specially-marked points evenly spaced on a line.
    a. Thing
    b. Number line0
    c. Undefined
    d. Undefined

42. A _____ is a numeral used to indicate a count. The most common use of the word today is to name the part of a fraction that tells the number or count of equal parts.
    a. Thing
    b. Numerator0
    c. Undefined
    d. Undefined

43. In mathematics, a _____ may be described informally as a number that can be given by an infinite decimal representation.
    a. Real number0
    b. Thing
    c. Undefined
    d. Undefined

44. Generally, a _____ is a splitting of something into parts.
    a. Partition0
    b. Thing
    c. Undefined
    d. Undefined

45. Acid _____ ratio measures the ability of a company to use its near cash or quick assets to immediately extinguish its current liabilities.
    a. Test0
    b. Thing
    c. Undefined
    d. Undefined

46. Mathematical _____ is used to represent ideas.
    a. Thing
    b. Notation0
    c. Undefined
    d. Undefined

47. _____ is the notation in which permitted values for a variable are expressed as ranging over a certain interval; "5 < x < 9" is an example of the application of _____.
    a. Interval notation0
    b. Thing
    c. Undefined
    d. Undefined

Chapter 4. Graphing and Optimization

48. A _____ defined function f(x) of a real variable x is a function whose definition is given differently on disjoint subsets of its domain.
   a. Piecewise0
   b. Thing
   c. Undefined
   d. Undefined

49. A _____ is a fee added to a customer's bill.
   a. Service charge0
   b. Thing
   c. Undefined
   d. Undefined

50. _____ are a measure of time.
   a. Thing
   b. Minutes0
   c. Undefined
   d. Undefined

51. A _____ is a special kind of ratio, indicating a relationship between two measurements with different units, such as miles to gallons or cents to pounds.
   a. Rate0
   b. Thing
   c. Undefined
   d. Undefined

52. _____ is a kind of property which exists as magnitude or multitude. It is among the basic classes of things along with quality, substance, change, and relation.
   a. Thing
   b. Amount0
   c. Undefined
   d. Undefined

53. _____ is a temperature scale named after the German physicist Daniel Gabriel _____ , who proposed it in 1724.
   a. Thing
   b. Fahrenheit0
   c. Undefined
   d. Undefined

54. The _____ .
   a. British thermal unit0
   b. Thing
   c. Undefined
   d. Undefined

55. In mathematics, there are several meanings of _____ depending on the subject.
   a. Degree0
   b. Thing
   c. Undefined
   d. Undefined

56. _____ is a form of periodic payment from an employer to an employee, which is specified in an employment contract.
   a. Thing
   b. Gross pay0
   c. Undefined
   d. Undefined

57. The payment of _____ as remuneration for services rendered or products sold is a common way to reward sales people.
   a. Thing
   b. Commission0
   c. Undefined
   d. Undefined

Chapter 4. Graphing and Optimization

58. A _____ is a form of periodic payment from an employer to an employee, which is specified in an employment contract.
   a. Thing
   b. Salary0
   c. Undefined
   d. Undefined

59. There are two simple _____ the greatest common factor and least common multiple: standard factorization and prime factorization.
   a. Thing
   b. Methods for finding0
   c. Undefined
   d. Undefined

60. _____ is the application of tools and a processing medium to the transformation of raw materials into finished goods for sale.
   a. Manufacturing0
   b. Thing
   c. Undefined
   d. Undefined

61. _____ is often used to describe the measurement of the steepness, incline, gradient, or grade of a straight line. The _____ is defined as the ratio of the "rise" divided by the "run" between two points on a line, or in other words, the ratio of the altitude change to the horizontal distance between any two points on the line.
   a. Slope0
   b. Thing
   c. Undefined
   d. Undefined

62. In trigonometry, the _____ is a function defined as $\tan x = \sin x / \cos x$. The function is so-named because it can be defined as the length of a certain segment of a _____ (in the geometric sense) to the unit circle. In plane geometry, a line is _____ to a curve, at some point, if both line and curve pass through the point with the same direction.
   a. Thing
   b. Tangent0
   c. Undefined
   d. Undefined

63. _____ has two distinct but etymologically-related meanings: one in geometry and one in trigonometry.
   a. Tangent line0
   b. Thing
   c. Undefined
   d. Undefined

64. In astronomy, geography, geometry and related sciences and contexts, a plane is said to be _____ at a given point if it is locally perpendicular to the gradient of the gravity field, i.e., with the direction of the gravitational force at that point.
   a. Thing
   b. Horizontal0
   c. Undefined
   d. Undefined

65. _____ is an adjective usually refering to being in the centre.
   a. Central0
   b. Thing
   c. Undefined
   d. Undefined

66. In mathematics, defined and _____ are used to explain whether or not expressions have meaningful, sensible, and unambiguous values.
   a. Undefined0
   b. Thing
   c. Undefined
   d. Undefined

Chapter 4. Graphing and Optimization

67. In mathematics, a _____ of a k-place relation $L \subseteq X_1 \times ... \times X_k$ is one of the sets X_j, $1 \leq j \leq k$. In the special case where k = 2 and $L \subseteq X_1 \times X_2$ is a function $L : X_1 \to X_2$, it is conventional to refer to X_1 as the _____ of the function and to refer to X_2 as the codomain of the function.
   a. Thing
   b. Domain0
   c. Undefined
   d. Undefined

68. A _____ is a set whose members are members of another set or a set contained within another set.
   a. Thing
   b. Subset0
   c. Undefined
   d. Undefined

69. _____ are groups whose members are members of another set or a set contained within another set.
   a. Thing
   b. Subsets0
   c. Undefined
   d. Undefined

70. A _____ is a function for which, intuitively, small changes in the input result in small changes in the output.
   a. Continuous function0
   b. Event
   c. Undefined
   d. Undefined

71. in mathematics, maxima and minima, known collectively as _____, are the largest value maximum or smallest value minimum, that a function takes in a point either within a given neighborhood or on the function domain in its entirety global extremum.
   a. Thing
   b. Extrema0
   c. Undefined
   d. Undefined

72. A real-valued function f defined on the real line is said to have a _____ point at the point $x*$, if there exists some $\varepsilon > 0$, such that f when $x - x* < \varepsilon$.
   a. Local maximum0
   b. Thing
   c. Undefined
   d. Undefined

73. In mathematics, maxima and minima, known collectively as extrema, are the largest value maximum or smallest value minimum, that a function takes in a point either within a given neighborhood local _____ or on the function domain in its entirety global _____.
   a. Thing
   b. Extremum0
   c. Undefined
   d. Undefined

74. In mathematics, a _____ of a complex-valued function f is a member x of the domain of f such that f(x) vanishes at x, that is, $x : f(x) = 0$.
   a. Thing
   b. Root0
   c. Undefined
   d. Undefined

75. Any point where a graph makes contact with an coordinate axis is called an _____ of the graph
   a. Thing
   b. Intercept0
   c. Undefined
   d. Undefined

76. In mathematics, a _____ is the result of multiplying, or an expression that identifies factors to be multiplied.

Chapter 4. Graphing and Optimization

a. Product0
b. Thing
c. Undefined
d. Undefined

77. In banking and accountancy, the outstanding _____ is the amount of money owned, or due, that remains in a deposit account or a loan account at a given date, after all past remittances, payments and withdrawal have been accounted for.
a. Balance0
b. Thing
c. Undefined
d. Undefined

78. _____ is the difference between the monetary value of exports and imports in an economy over a certain period of time.
a. Thing
b. Trade balance0
c. Undefined
d. Undefined

79. _____ is the extra revenue that an additional unit of product will bring a firm. It can also be described as the change in total revenue/change in number of units sold.
a. Thing
b. Marginal revenue0
c. Undefined
d. Undefined

80. _____ is a business term for the amount of money that a company receives from its activities in a given period, mostly from sales of products and/or services to customers
a. Revenue0
b. Thing
c. Undefined
d. Undefined

81. A _____ is a set of numbers that designate location in a given reference system, such as x,y in a planar _____ system or an x,y,z in a three-dimensional _____ system.
a. Thing
b. Coordinate0
c. Undefined
d. Undefined

82. In mathematics, an _____, mean, or central tendency of a data set refers to a measure of the "middle" or "expected" value of the data set.
a. Average0
b. Concept
c. Undefined
d. Undefined

83. _____ is the change in total cost that arises when the quantity produced changes by one unit.
a. Marginal cost0
b. Thing
c. Undefined
d. Undefined

84. _____ is the use of marginal concepts within economics. Marginal concepts include marginal cost, marginal productivity and marginal utility, the law of diminishing rates of substitution, and the law of diminishing marginal utility.
a. Marginal analysis0
b. Thing
c. Undefined
d. Undefined

85. _____ is a a point on a curve at which the tangent crosses the curve itself.

a. Inflection point0
b. Thing
c. Undefined
d. Undefined

86. The word _____ means curving in or hollowed inward.
a. Thing
b. Concavity0
c. Undefined
d. Undefined

87. In mathematics and its applications, a _____ is a system for assigning an n-tuple of numbers or scalars to each point in an n-dimensional space.
a. Coordinate system0
b. Concept
c. Undefined
d. Undefined

88. _____ determines whether a given critical point of a function is a maximum, a minimum, or neither.
a. Thing
b. First Derivative Test0
c. Undefined
d. Undefined

89. A _____ is an individual or household that purchases and uses goods and services generated within the economy.
a. Consumer0
b. Thing
c. Undefined
d. Undefined

90. _____ is a statistical time-series measure of a weighted average of prices of a specified set of goods and services purchased by consumers
a. Thing
b. Consumer price index0
c. Undefined
d. Undefined

91. The word _____ is used in a variety of ways in mathematics.
a. Index0
b. Thing
c. Undefined
d. Undefined

92. In mainstream economics, the word _____ refers to a general rise in prices measured against a standard level of purchasing power.
a. Inflation0
b. Thing
c. Undefined
d. Undefined

93. A _____ is a function that assigns a number to subsets of a given set.
a. Measure0
b. Thing
c. Undefined
d. Undefined

94. _____ is a synonym for information.
a. Thing
b. Data0
c. Undefined
d. Undefined

95. Multiple Signal Classification, also known as _____, is an algorithm used for frequency estimation and emitter location.

a. Thing
b. Music0
c. Undefined
d. Undefined

96. An _____ or member of a set is an object that when collected together make up the set.
a. Thing
b. Element0
c. Undefined
d. Undefined

97. _____ is the state of being greater than any finite number, however large.
a. Thing
b. Infinity0
c. Undefined
d. Undefined

98. In mathematics, the _____ (or modulus) of a real number is its numerical value without regard to its sign.
a. Absolute value0
b. Thing
c. Undefined
d. Undefined

99. _____ has many meanings, most of which simply .
a. Thing
b. Power0
c. Undefined
d. Undefined

100. In mathematics, the multiplicative inverse of a number x, denoted 1/x or x^{-1}, is the number which, when multiplied by x, yields 1. The multiplicative inverse of x is also called the _____ of x.
a. Thing
b. Reciprocal0
c. Undefined
d. Undefined

101. A _____ is a quantity that denotes the proportional amount or magnitude of one quantity relative to another.
a. Ratio0
b. Thing
c. Undefined
d. Undefined

102. In calculus and other branches of mathematical analysis, an _____ is an algebraic expression obtained in the context of limits.
a. Thing
b. Indeterminate form0
c. Undefined
d. Undefined

103. In mathematics, _____ is the decomposition of an object into a product of other objects, or factors, which when multiplied together give the original.
a. Thing
b. Factoring0
c. Undefined
d. Undefined

104. The term _____ refers to the largest and the smallest element of a set.
a. Extreme value0
b. Thing
c. Undefined
d. Undefined

105. In geometry, an _____ is a point at which a line segment or ray terminates.
a. Endpoint0
b. Thing
c. Undefined
d. Undefined

Chapter 4. Graphing and Optimization

106. A _____ is a negotiable instrument instructing a financial institution to pay a specific amount of a specific currency from a specific demand account held in the maker/depositor's name with that institution. Both the maker and payee may be natural persons or legal entities.
   a. Thing
   b. Check0
   c. Undefined
   d. Undefined

107. A _____ is a symbolic representation denoting a quantity or expression. It often represents an "unknown" quantity that has the potential to change.
   a. Thing
   b. Variable0
   c. Undefined
   d. Undefined

108. A _____ is an abstract model that uses mathematical language to describe the behavior of a system. Eykhoff defined a _____ as 'a representation of the essential aspects of an existing system which presents knowledge of that system in usable form'.
   a. Mathematical model0
   b. Thing
   c. Undefined
   d. Undefined

109. In mathematics, _____ are the intuitive idea of a geometrical one-dimensional and continuous object.
   a. Curves0
   b. Thing
   c. Undefined
   d. Undefined

110. In mathematics, _____ refers to the rewriting of an expression into a simpler form.
   a. Thing
   b. Reduction0
   c. Undefined
   d. Undefined

111. In mathematics and logic, a _____ proof is a way of showing the truth or falsehood of a given statement by a straightforward combination of established facts, usually existing lemmas and theorems, without making any further assumptions.
   a. Direct0
   b. Thing
   c. Undefined
   d. Undefined

112. An _____ is a combination of numbers, operators, grouping symbols and/or free variables and bound variables arranged in a meaningful way which can be evaluated..
   a. Thing
   b. Expression0
   c. Undefined
   d. Undefined

113. In finance, a _____ is collateral that the holder of a position in securities, options, or futures contracts has to deposit to cover the credit risk of his counterparty.
   a. Margin0
   b. Thing
   c. Undefined
   d. Undefined

114. In economics, supply and _____ describe market relations between prospective sellers and buyers of a good.
   a. Thing
   b. Demand0
   c. Undefined
   d. Undefined

Chapter 4. Graphing and Optimization

115. A _____ is the result of the addition of a set of numbers. The numbers may be natural numbers, complex numbers, matrices, or still more complicated objects. An infinite _____ is a subtle procedure known as a series.
    a. Sum0
    b. Thing
    c. Undefined
    d. Undefined

116. In geometry, a _____ is defined as a quadrilateral where all four of its angles are right angles.
    a. Thing
    b. Rectangle0
    c. Undefined
    d. Undefined

117. _____ is the distance around a given two-dimensional object. As a general rule, the _____ of a polygon can always be calculated by adding all the length of the sides together. So, the formula for triangles is P = a + b + c, where a, b and c stand for each side of it. For quadrilaterals the equation is P = a + b + c + d. For equilateral polygons, P = na, where n is the number of sides and a is the side length.
    a. Thing
    b. Perimeter0
    c. Undefined
    d. Undefined

118. In plane geometry, a _____ is a polygon with four equal sides, four right angles, and parallel opposite sides. In algebra, the _____ of a number is that number multiplied by itself.
    a. Thing
    b. Square0
    c. Undefined
    d. Undefined

119. In logic and mathematics, logical _____ is a logical relation that holds between a set T of formulas and a formula B when every model (or interpretation or valuation) of T is also a model of B.
    a. Concept
    b. Implication0
    c. Undefined
    d. Undefined

120. In mathematics, an _____ is any of the arguments, i.e. "inputs", to a function. Thus if we have a function f(x), then x is a _____.
    a. Independent variable0
    b. Thing
    c. Undefined
    d. Undefined

121. The word _____ comes from the Latin word linearis, which means created by lines.
    a. Linear0
    b. Thing
    c. Undefined
    d. Undefined

122. _____ is a regression method that models the relationship between a dependent variable Y, independent variables Xp, and a random term à.
    a. Linear regression0
    b. Thing
    c. Undefined
    d. Undefined

123. _____ is the ability to hold, receive or absorb, or a measure thereof, similar to the concept of volume.
    a. Capacity0
    b. Concept
    c. Undefined
    d. Undefined

124. The _____ of a solid object is the three-dimensional concept of how much space it occupies, often quantified numerically.

Chapter 4. Graphing and Optimization

a. Volume0
b. Thing
c. Undefined
d. Undefined

125. In classical geometry, a _____ of a circle or sphere is any line segment from its center to its boundary. By extension, the _____ of a circle or sphere is the length of any such segment. The _____ is half the diameter. In science and engineering the term _____ of curvature is commonly used as a synonym for _____.
a. Thing
b. Radius0
c. Undefined
d. Undefined

126. In geometry, _____ angles are angles that have a common ray coming out of the vertex going between two other rays.
a. Concept
b. Adjacent0
c. Undefined
d. Undefined

127. A _____ is a unit of length, usually used to measure distance, in a number of different systems, including Imperial units, United States customary units and Norwegian/Swedish mil. Its size can vary from system to system, but in each is between 1 and 10 kilometers. In contemporary English contexts _____ refers to either:
a. Thing
b. Mile0
c. Undefined
d. Undefined

128. _____ is a unit of speed, expressing the number of international miles covered per hour.
a. Miles per hour0
b. Thing
c. Undefined
d. Undefined

129. In mathematics, a _____ is a quadric surface, with the following equation in Cartesian coordinates: $(x/_a)^2 + (y/_b)^2 = 1$.
a. Cylinder0
b. Thing
c. Undefined
d. Undefined

130. _____ is the process in which two clone daughter cells are produced by the cell division of one bacterium.
a. Thing
b. Bacteria growth0
c. Undefined
d. Undefined

131. In sociology and biology a _____ is the collection of people or organisms of a particular species living in a given geographic area or space, usually measured by a census.
a. Thing
b. Population0
c. Undefined
d. Undefined

132. _____, in economics and political economy, are the distributions or payments awarded to the various suppliers of the factors of production.
a. Returns0
b. Thing
c. Undefined
d. Undefined

133. According to _____ relationship, in a production system with fixed and variable inputs, beyond some point, each additional unit of variable input yields less and less additional output.

Chapter 4. Graphing and Optimization

a. Diminishing returns0
b. Thing
c. Undefined
d. Undefined

134. In geometry, an _____ angle is an angle that is not a 90 degree angle, or an angle that is divisible by 90: 180, 270, 360/0

a. Thing
b. Oblique0
c. Undefined
d. Undefined

135. _____ are citizens in a democratic form of governance that have checked in with some form of a central registry, which in turn permits them to vote.

a. Thing
b. Registered voters0
c. Undefined
d. Undefined

136. _____ are procedures that allow people to exchange information by one of several methods.

a. Thing
b. Communications0
c. Undefined
d. Undefined

137. In mathematics, two quantities are called _____ if they vary in such a way that one of the quantities is a constant multiple of the other, or equivalently if they have a constant ratio.

a. Thing
b. Proportional0
c. Undefined
d. Undefined

Chapter 5. Additional Derivative Topics

1. A _____ function is a function for which, intuitively, small changes in the input result in small changes in the output.
   a. Continuous0
   b. Event
   c. Undefined
   d. Undefined

2. _____ is the fee paid on borrowed money.
   a. Thing
   b. Interest0
   c. Undefined
   d. Undefined

3. _____ interest refers to the fact that whenever interest is calculated, it is based not only on the original principal, but also on any unpaid interest that has been added to the principal.
   a. Compound0
   b. Thing
   c. Undefined
   d. Undefined

4. _____ refers to the fact that whenever interest is calculated, it is based not only on the original principal, but also on any unpaid interest that has been added to the principal. The more frequently interest is compounded, the faster the balance grows.
   a. Compound interest0
   b. Concept
   c. Undefined
   d. Undefined

5. In mathematics, _____ growth occurs when the growth rate of a function is always proportional to the function's current size.
   a. Thing
   b. Exponential0
   c. Undefined
   d. Undefined

6. In mathematics and the mathematical sciences, a _____ is a fixed, but possibly unspecified, value. This is in contrast to a variable, which is not fixed.
   a. Constant0
   b. Thing
   c. Undefined
   d. Undefined

7. The mathematical concept of a _____ expresses the intuitive idea of deterministic dependence between two quantities, one of which is viewed as primary and the other as secondary. A _____ then is a way to associate a unique output for each input of a specified type, for example, a real number or an element of a given set.
   a. Thing
   b. Function0
   c. Undefined
   d. Undefined

8. In mathematics, an _____ number is any real number that is not a rational number- that is, it is a number which cannot be expressed as a fraction m/n, where m and n are integers.
   a. Irrational0
   b. Thing
   c. Undefined
   d. Undefined

9. In mathematics, an _____ is any real number that is not a rational number ¡ª that is, it is a number which cannot be expressed as m/n, where m and n are integers.
   a. Irrational number0
   b. Thing
   c. Undefined
   d. Undefined

10. An _____ is a combination of numbers, operators, grouping symbols and/or free variables and bound variables arranged in a meaningful way which can be evaluated..

a. Thing
b. Expression0
c. Undefined
d. Undefined

11. In mathematics, a _____ is a demonstration that, assuming certain axioms, some statement is necessarily true.
a. Thing
b. Proof0
c. Undefined
d. Undefined

12. _____ has many meanings, most of which simply .
a. Power0
b. Thing
c. Undefined
d. Undefined

13. Leonhard _____ was a pioneering Swiss mathematician and physicist, who spent most of his life in Russia and Germany.
a. Person
b. Euler0
c. Undefined
d. Undefined

14. _____ was a pioneering Swiss mathematician and physicist, who spent most of his life in Russia and Germany.
a. Leonhard Euler0
b. Person
c. Undefined
d. Undefined

15. A _____ is a special kind of ratio, indicating a relationship between two measurements with different units, such as miles to gallons or cents to pounds.
a. Thing
b. Rate0
c. Undefined
d. Undefined

16. Equivalence is the condition of being _____ or essentially equal.
a. Thing
b. Equivalent0
c. Undefined
d. Undefined

17. _____ is a kind of property which exists as magnitude or multitude. It is among the basic classes of things along with quality, substance, change, and relation.
a. Amount0
b. Thing
c. Undefined
d. Undefined

18. An _____ is the fee paid on borrow money.
a. Interest rate0
b. Concept
c. Undefined
d. Undefined

19. A _____ is 360° or 2∂ radians.
a. Thing
b. Turn0
c. Undefined
d. Undefined

20. In mathematics, a _____ may be described informally as a number that can be given by an infinite decimal representation.

a. Real number0
b. Thing
c. Undefined
d. Undefined

21. In set theory and other branches of mathematics, the _____ of a collection of sets is the set that contains everything that belongs to any of the sets, but nothing else.
a. Union0
b. Thing
c. Undefined
d. Undefined

22. A _____ or CD is a time deposit, a financial product commonly offered to consumers by banks, thrift institutions, and credit unions.
a. Thing
b. Certificate of deposit0
c. Undefined
d. Undefined

23. _____ or investing is a term with several closely-related meanings in business management, finance and economics, related to saving or deferring consumption.
a. Thing
b. Investment0
c. Undefined
d. Undefined

24. In business, particularly accounting, a _____ is the time intervals that the accounts, statement, payments, or other calculations cover.
a. Thing
b. Period0
c. Undefined
d. Undefined

25. _____ generally derives from name. A _____ quantity e.g., length, diameter, volume, voltage, value is generally the quantity according to which some item has been named or is generally referred to.
a. Thing
b. Nominal0
c. Undefined
d. Undefined

26. The _____, the average in everyday English, which is also called the arithmetic _____ (and is distinguished from the geometric _____ or harmonic _____). The average is also called the sample _____. The expected value of a random variable, which is also called the population _____.
a. Mean0
b. Thing
c. Undefined
d. Undefined

27. _____ is the logarithm to the base e, where e is an irrational constant approximately equal to 2.718281828459.
a. Thing
b. Natural logarithm0
c. Undefined
d. Undefined

28. In mathematics, a _____ of a number x is the exponent y of the power by such that $x = b^y$. The value used for the base b must be neither 0 nor 1, nor a root of 1 in the case of the extension to complex numbers, and is typically 10, e, or 2.
a. Thing
b. Logarithm0
c. Undefined
d. Undefined

29. Two mathematical objects are equal if and only if they are precisely the same in every way. This defines a binary relation, _____, denoted by the sign of _____ "=" in such a way that the statement "x = y" means that x and y are equal.

Chapter 5. Additional Derivative Topics

a. Equality0
b. Thing
c. Undefined
d. Undefined

30. _____ of a single or multiple future payments is the nominal amounts of money to change hands at some future date, discounted to account for the time value of money, and other factors such as investment risk.
   a. Thing
   b. Present value0
   c. Undefined
   d. Undefined

31. _____ is the process in which an unstable atomic nucleus loses energy by emitting radiation in the form of particles or electromagnetic waves.
   a. Radioactive decay0
   b. Thing
   c. Undefined
   d. Undefined

32. The _____ is the total number of human beings alive on the planet Earth at a given time.
   a. World population0
   b. Thing
   c. Undefined
   d. Undefined

33. In sociology and biology a _____ is the collection of people or organisms of a particular species living in a given geographic area or space, usually measured by a census.
   a. Population0
   b. Thing
   c. Undefined
   d. Undefined

34. The _____ is the period of time required for a quantity to double in size or value.
   a. Thing
   b. Doubling time0
   c. Undefined
   d. Undefined

35. _____ is change in population over time, and can be quantified as the change in the number of individuals in a population per unit time.
   a. Thing
   b. Population growth0
   c. Undefined
   d. Undefined

36. The _____ is a measurement of how a function changes when the values of its inputs change.
   a. Derivative0
   b. Thing
   c. Undefined
   d. Undefined

37. In mathematics, a _____ is the end result of a division problem. It can also be expressed as the number of times the divisor divides into the dividend.
   a. Thing
   b. Quotient0
   c. Undefined
   d. Undefined

38. The function difference divided by the point difference is known as the _____
   a. Difference quotient0
   b. Thing
   c. Undefined
   d. Undefined

39. _____ is one of the most important functions in mathematics. A function commonly used to study growth and decay

Chapter 5. Additional Derivative Topics

a. Thing
c. Undefined
b. Exponential function0
d. Undefined

40. _____ is a method for differentiating expressions involving exponentiation the power operation.
    a. Power rule0
    b. Thing
    c. Undefined
    d. Undefined

41. A _____ is a symbolic representation denoting a quantity or expression. It often represents an "unknown" quantity that has the potential to change.
    a. Variable0
    b. Thing
    c. Undefined
    d. Undefined

42. _____ is a straight line or curve A to which another curve B the one being studied approaches closer and closer as one moves along it.
    a. Thing
    b. Vertical asymptote0
    c. Undefined
    d. Undefined

43. An _____ is a straight line or curve A to which another curve B approaches closer and closer as one moves along it. As one moves along B, the space between it and the _____ A becomes smaller and smaller, and can in fact be made as small as one could wish by going far enough along. A curve may or may not touch or cross its _____. In fact, the curve may intersect the _____ an infinite number of times.
    a. Asymptote0
    b. Thing
    c. Undefined
    d. Undefined

44. An _____ is a straight line around which a geometric figure can be rotated.
    a. Thing
    b. Axis0
    c. Undefined
    d. Undefined

45. In astronomy, geography, geometry and related sciences and contexts, a plane is said to be _____ at a given point if it is locally perpendicular to the gradient of the gravity field, i.e., with the direction of the gravitational force at that point.
    a. Horizontal0
    b. Thing
    c. Undefined
    d. Undefined

46. _____ are the basic objects of study in graph theory. Informally speaking, a graph is a set of objects called points, nodes, or vertices connected by links called lines or edges.
    a. Graphs0
    b. Thing
    c. Undefined
    d. Undefined

47. Any point where a graph makes contact with an coordinate axis is called an _____ of the graph
    a. Intercept0
    b. Thing
    c. Undefined
    d. Undefined

48. In mathematics, a _____ of a k-place relation $L \subseteq X_1 \times ... \times X_k$ is one of the sets X_j, $1 \leq j \leq k$. In the special case where k = 2 and $L \subseteq X_1 \times X_2$ is a function $L : X_1 \to X_2$, it is conventional to refer to X_1 as the _____ of the function and to refer to X_2 as the codomain of the function.

Chapter 5. Additional Derivative Topics

a. Domain0
b. Thing
c. Undefined
d. Undefined

49. _____, from Latin meaning "to make progress", is defined in two different ways. Pure economic _____ is the increase in wealth that an investor has from making an investment, taking into consideration all costs associated with that investment including the opportunity cost of capital.
   a. Thing
   b. Profit0
   c. Undefined
   d. Undefined

50. Acid _____ ratio measures the ability of a company to use its near cash or quick assets to immediately extinguish its current liabilities.
   a. Thing
   b. Test0
   c. Undefined
   d. Undefined

51. A _____ is a negotiable instrument instructing a financial institution to pay a specific amount of a specific currency from a specific demand account held in the maker/depositor's name with that institution. Both the maker and payee may be natural persons or legal entities.
   a. Check0
   b. Thing
   c. Undefined
   d. Undefined

52. In trigonometry, the _____ is a function defined as $\tan x = \sin x / \cos x$. The function is so-named because it can be defined as the length of a certain segment of a _____ (in the geometric sense) to the unit circle. In plane geometry, a line is _____ to a curve, at some point, if both line and curve pass through the point with the same direction.
   a. Thing
   b. Tangent0
   c. Undefined
   d. Undefined

53. in mathematics, maxima and minima, known collectively as _____, are the largest value maximum or smallest value minimum, that a function takes in a point either within a given neighborhood or on the function domain in its entirety global extremum.
   a. Extrema0
   b. Thing
   c. Undefined
   d. Undefined

54. In elementary algebra, an _____ is a set that contains every real number between two indicated numbers and may contain the two numbers themselves.
   a. Interval0
   b. Thing
   c. Undefined
   d. Undefined

55. In mathematics, an inequality is a statement about the relative size or order of two objects. For example 14 > 10, or 14 is _____ 10.
   a. Thing
   b. Greater than0
   c. Undefined
   d. Undefined

56. In mathematics, the _____ of two sets A and B is the set that contains all elements of A that also belong to B (or equivalently, all elements of B that also belong to A), but no other elements.

Chapter 5. Additional Derivative Topics

a. Intersection0
b. Thing
c. Undefined
d. Undefined

57. In probability theory, _____ are various sets of outcomes (a subset of the sample space) to which a probability is assigned.
    a. Thing
    b. Events0
    c. Undefined
    d. Undefined

58. In economics, supply and _____ describe market relations between prospective sellers and buyers of a good.
    a. Demand0
    b. Thing
    c. Undefined
    d. Undefined

59. In mathematics, the conjugate _____ or adjoint matrix of an m-by-n matrix A with complex entries is the n-by-m matrix A* obtained from A by taking the transpose and then taking the complex conjugate of each entry.
    a. Thing
    b. Pairs0
    c. Undefined
    d. Undefined

60. In mathematics, an _____, mean, or central tendency of a data set refers to a measure of the "middle" or "expected" value of the data set.
    a. Average0
    b. Concept
    c. Undefined
    d. Undefined

61. In mathematics, a _____ is the result of multiplying, or an expression that identifies factors to be multiplied.
    a. Product0
    b. Thing
    c. Undefined
    d. Undefined

62. The _____ of measurement are a globally standardized and modernized form of the metric system.
    a. Thing
    b. Units0
    c. Undefined
    d. Undefined

63. _____ is a business term for the amount of money that a company receives from its activities in a given period, mostly from sales of products and/or services to customers
    a. Revenue0
    b. Thing
    c. Undefined
    d. Undefined

64. In the scientific method, an _____ (Latin: ex-+-periri, "of (or from) trying"), is a set of actions and observations, performed in the context of solving a particular problem or question, in order to support or falsify a hypothesis or research concerning phenomena.
    a. Thing
    b. Experiment0
    c. Undefined
    d. Undefined

65. In calculus, the _____ is a formula for the derivative of the composite of two functions.
    a. Chain rule0
    b. Concept
    c. Undefined
    d. Undefined

66. In mathematics, a _____ of a positive integer n is a way of writing n as a sum of positive integers.

Chapter 5. Additional Derivative Topics

a. Thing
c. Undefined
b. Composition0
d. Undefined

67. A _____ number is a positive integer which has a positive divisor other than one or itself.
a. Composite0
c. Undefined
b. Thing
d. Undefined

68. In mathematics, a _____ is an expression that is constructed from one or more variables and constants, using only the operations of addition, subtraction, multiplication, and constant positive whole number exponents. is a _____. Note in particular that division by an expression containing a variable is not in general allowed in polynomials. [1]
a. Polynomial0
c. Undefined
b. Thing
d. Undefined

69. A _____, formed by the composition of one function on another, represents the application of the former to the result of the application of the latter to the argument of the composite.
a. Composite function0
c. Undefined
b. Thing
d. Undefined

70. In economics _____ means before deductions brutto, e.g. _____ domestic or national product, or _____ profit or income
a. Thing
c. Undefined
b. Gross0
d. Undefined

71. In differential calculus, _____ problems involve finding the rate at which a quantity is changing by relating that quantity to other quantities whose rates of change are known.
a. Thing
c. Undefined
b. Related rates0
d. Undefined

72. _____ is a relation in Euclidean geometry among the three sides of a right triangle.
a. Pythagorean Theorem0
c. Undefined
b. Thing
d. Undefined

73. In mathematics, a _____ is a statement that can be proved on the basis of explicitly stated or previously agreed assumptions.
a. Theorem0
c. Undefined
b. Thing
d. Undefined

74. A _____ is a unit of length, usually used to measure distance, in a number of different systems, including Imperial units, United States customary units and Norwegian/Swedish mil. Its size can vary from system to system, but in each is between 1 and 10 kilometers. In contemporary English contexts _____ refers to either:
a. Thing
c. Undefined
b. Mile0
d. Undefined

75. _____ is a unit of speed, expressing the number of international miles covered per hour.

Chapter 5. Additional Derivative Topics

a. Miles per hour0   b. Thing
c. Undefined   d. Undefined

76. A _____ is a set of numbers that designate location in a given reference system, such as x,y in a planar _____ system or an x,y,z in a three-dimensional _____ system.
a. Coordinate0   b. Thing
c. Undefined   d. Undefined

77. In classical geometry, a _____ of a circle or sphere is any line segment from its center to its boundary. By extension, the _____ of a circle or sphere is the length of any such segment. The _____ is half the diameter. In science and engineering the term _____ of curvature is commonly used as a synonym for _____.
a. Radius0   b. Thing
c. Undefined   d. Undefined

78. The _____ of a solid object is the three-dimensional concept of how much space it occupies, often quantified numerically.
a. Thing   b. Volume0
c. Undefined   d. Undefined

79. _____ is a physical property of a system that underlies the common notions of hot and cold; something that is hotter has the greater _____.
a. Temperature0   b. Thing
c. Undefined   d. Undefined

80. The _____ rule, also known as a slipstick, is a mechanical analog computer, consisting of at least two finely divided scales, most often a fixed outer pair and a movable inner one, with a sliding window called the cursor.
a. Slide0   b. Thing
c. Undefined   d. Undefined

81. A _____ is one of the basic shapes of geometry: a polygon with three vertices and three sides which are straight line segments.
a. Triangle0   b. Thing
c. Undefined   d. Undefined

82. The _____ of a right triangle is the triangle's longest side; the side opposite the right angle.
a. Thing   b. Hypotenuse0
c. Undefined   d. Undefined

83. _____ has one 90° internal angle a right angle.
a. Thing   b. Right triangle0
c. Undefined   d. Undefined

84. The metre (or _____, see spelling differences) is a measure of length. It is the basic unit of length in the metric system and in the International System of Units (SI), used around the world for general and scientific purposes.

Chapter 5. Additional Derivative Topics

a. Meter0
b. Concept
c. Undefined
d. Undefined

85. _____ are a measure of time.
   a. Minutes0
   b. Thing
   c. Undefined
   d. Undefined

86. One of the three formats applicable to a quadratic function is the _____ which is defined as f = ax² + bx + c.
   a. Thing
   b. General form0
   c. Undefined
   d. Undefined

87. _____ is to give an equation R(x,y) = S(x,y) that at least in part has the same graph as y = f(x).
   a. Implicit differentiation0
   b. Thing
   c. Undefined
   d. Undefined

88. _____, a field in mathematics, is the study of how functions change when their inputs change. The primary object of study in _____ is the derivative.
   a. Differential calculus0
   b. Thing
   c. Undefined
   d. Undefined

89. Mathematical _____ is used to represent ideas.
   a. Notation0
   b. Thing
   c. Undefined
   d. Undefined

90. In plane geometry, a _____ is a polygon with four equal sides, four right angles, and parallel opposite sides. In algebra, the _____ of a number is that number multiplied by itself.
   a. Thing
   b. Square0
   c. Undefined
   d. Undefined

91. _____ is the use of marginal concepts within economics. Marginal concepts include marginal cost, marginal productivity and marginal utility, the law of diminishing rates of substitution, and the law of diminishing marginal utility.
   a. Marginal analysis0
   b. Thing
   c. Undefined
   d. Undefined

92. _____ is the application of tools and a processing medium to the transformation of raw materials into finished goods for sale.
   a. Thing
   b. Manufacturing0
   c. Undefined
   d. Undefined

93. In economics and business studies, the _____ is an elasticity that measures the nature and degree of the relationship between changes in quantity demanded of a good and changes in its price.
   a. Elasticity of demand0
   b. Thing
   c. Undefined
   d. Undefined

94. A _____ is a function that assigns a number to subsets of a given set.

Chapter 5. Additional Derivative Topics

a. Measure0
b. Thing
c. Undefined
d. Undefined

95. _____, in economics and political economy, are the distributions or payments awarded to the various suppliers of the factors of production.
   a. Thing
   b. Returns0
   c. Undefined
   d. Undefined

96. According to _____ relationship, in a production system with fixed and variable inputs, beyond some point, each additional unit of variable input yields less and less additional output.
   a. Diminishing returns0
   b. Thing
   c. Undefined
   d. Undefined

Chapter 6. Integration

1. _____ is an extension of the concept of a sum.
   a. Definite integral0
   b. Thing
   c. Undefined
   d. Undefined

2. The _____ of a function is an extension of the concept of a sum, and are identified or found through the use of integration.
   a. Thing
   b. Integral0
   c. Undefined
   d. Undefined

3. An _____ of a function f is a function F whose derivative is equal to f, i.e., F' = f.
   a. Thing
   b. Antiderivative0
   c. Undefined
   d. Undefined

4. The _____ is a measurement of how a function changes when the values of its inputs change.
   a. Derivative0
   b. Thing
   c. Undefined
   d. Undefined

5. The mathematical concept of a _____ expresses the intuitive idea of deterministic dependence between two quantities, one of which is viewed as primary and the other as secondary. A _____ then is a way to associate a unique output for each input of a specified type, for example, a real number or an element of a given set.
   a. Function0
   b. Thing
   c. Undefined
   d. Undefined

6. In mathematics, a _____ is a demonstration that, assuming certain axioms, some statement is necessarily true.
   a. Thing
   b. Proof0
   c. Undefined
   d. Undefined

7. In mathematics, a _____ is a statement that can be proved on the basis of explicitly stated or previously agreed assumptions.
   a. Thing
   b. Theorem0
   c. Undefined
   d. Undefined

8. In mathematics and the mathematical sciences, a _____ is a fixed, but possibly unspecified, value. This is in contrast to a variable, which is not fixed.
   a. Constant0
   b. Thing
   c. Undefined
   d. Undefined

9. In elementary algebra, an _____ is a set that contains every real number between two indicated numbers and may contain the two numbers themselves.
   a. Thing
   b. Interval0
   c. Undefined
   d. Undefined

10. The _____ of a ring R is defined to be the smallest positive integer n such that $na = 0$, for all a in R.
    a. Thing
    b. Characteristic0
    c. Undefined
    d. Undefined

Chapter 6. Integration

11. A _____ is a symbolic representation denoting a quantity or expression. It often represents an "unknown" quantity that has the potential to change.
    a. Thing
    b. Variable0
    c. Undefined
    d. Undefined

12. _____ in calculus is primitive or indefinite integral of a function f is a function F whose derivative is equal to f, i.e., F Œ = f. The process of solving for antiderivatives is _____
    a. Antidifferentiation0
    b. Thing
    c. Undefined
    d. Undefined

13. _____ is a process of combining or accumulating. It may also refer to:
    a. Thing
    b. Integration0
    c. Undefined
    d. Undefined

14. In calculus, the indefinite integral of a given function i.e. the set of all antiderivatives of the function is always written with a constant, the _____.
    a. Thing
    b. Constant of integration0
    c. Undefined
    d. Undefined

15. _____ is a function that extends the concept of an ordinary sum
    a. Integrand0
    b. Thing
    c. Undefined
    d. Undefined

16. In mathematics, a _____ may be described informally as a number that can be given by an infinite decimal representation.
    a. Thing
    b. Real number0
    c. Undefined
    d. Undefined

17. In mathematics, _____ growth occurs when the growth rate of a function is always proportional to the function's current size.
    a. Thing
    b. Exponential0
    c. Undefined
    d. Undefined

18. _____ is often used to describe the measurement of the steepness, incline, gradient, or grade of a straight line. The _____ is defined as the ratio of the "rise" divided by the "run" between two points on a line, or in other words, the ratio of the altitude change to the horizontal distance between any two points on the line.
    a. Thing
    b. Slope0
    c. Undefined
    d. Undefined

19. In mathematics, the concept of a _____ tries to capture the intuitive idea of a geometrical one-dimensional and continuous object. A simple example is the circle.
    a. Thing
    b. Curve0
    c. Undefined
    d. Undefined

20. In mathematics, _____ are the intuitive idea of a geometrical one-dimensional and continuous object.

Chapter 6. Integration

    a. Thing   b. Curves0
    c. Undefined   d. Undefined

21. In mathematics, the _____ f is the collection of all ordered pairs . In particular, graph means the graphical representation of this collection, in the form of a curve or surface, together with axes, etc. Graphing on a Cartesian plane is sometimes referred to as curve sketching.
    a. Graph of a function0   b. Thing
    c. Undefined   d. Undefined

22. _____ are the basic objects of study in graph theory. Informally speaking, a graph is a set of objects called points, nodes, or vertices connected by links called lines or edges.
    a. Thing   b. Graphs0
    c. Undefined   d. Undefined

23. A _____ is a special kind of ratio, indicating a relationship between two measurements with different units, such as miles to gallons or cents to pounds.
    a. Thing   b. Rate0
    c. Undefined   d. Undefined

24. In sociology and biology a _____ is the collection of people or organisms of a particular species living in a given geographic area or space, usually measured by a census.
    a. Population0   b. Thing
    c. Undefined   d. Undefined

25. _____ is change in population over time, and can be quantified as the change in the number of individuals in a population per unit time.
    a. Thing   b. Population growth0
    c. Undefined   d. Undefined

26. In a function the _____, is the variable which is the value, i.e. the "output", of the function.
    a. Thing   b. Dependent variable0
    c. Undefined   d. Undefined

27. The _____ of measurement are a globally standardized and modernized form of the metric system.
    a. Thing   b. Units0
    c. Undefined   d. Undefined

28. _____ is the change in total cost that arises when the quantity produced changes by one unit.
    a. Thing   b. Marginal cost0
    c. Undefined   d. Undefined

29. Fixed costs are expenses whose total does not change in proportion to the activity of a business. Unit fixed costs decline with volume following a retangular hyperbola as the volume of production. Variable costs by contrast change in relation to the activity of a business such as sales or production volume. Along with variable costs, fixed costs make up one of the two components of total cost. In the most simple production function total cost is equal to fixed costs plus variable costs. In accounting terminology, fixed costs will broadly include all costs which are not included in cost of goods sold, and variable costs are those captured in costs of goods sold. The implicit assumption required to make the equivalence between the accounting and economics terminology is that the accounting period is equal to the period in which fixed costs do not vary in relation to production. In practice, this equivalence does not always hold and depending on the period under consideration by management, some overhead expenses can be adjusted by management, and the specific allocation of each expense to each category will be decided under cost accounting. In business planning and management accounting, usage of the terms fixed costs, variable costs and others will often differ from usage in economics, and may depend on the intended use. For example, costs may be segregated into per unit costs fixed costs per period, and variable costs as a proportion of revenue. Capital expenditures will usually be allocated separately, and depending on the purpose, a portion may be regularly allocated to expenses as depreciation and amortization and seen as a _____ per period, or the entire amount may be considered upfront fixed costs.
   a. Fixed cost0
   b. Thing
   c. Undefined
   d. Undefined

30. In mathematics, the _____ of two sets A and B is the set that contains all elements of A that also belong to B (or equivalently, all elements of B that also belong to A), but no other elements.
   a. Intersection0
   b. Thing
   c. Undefined
   d. Undefined

31. _____ has many meanings, most of which simply .
   a. Power0
   b. Thing
   c. Undefined
   d. Undefined

32. _____ is a method for differentiating expressions involving exponentiation the power operation.
   a. Thing
   b. Power rule0
   c. Undefined
   d. Undefined

33. _____ is one of the most important functions in mathematics. A function commonly used to study growth and decay
   a. Thing
   b. Exponential function0
   c. Undefined
   d. Undefined

34. In mathematics, a _____ is the result of multiplying, or an expression that identifies factors to be multiplied.
   a. Thing
   b. Product0
   c. Undefined
   d. Undefined

35. In common philosophical language, a proposition or _____, is the content of an assertion, that is, it is true-or-false and defined by the meaning of a particular piece of language.
   a. Concept
   b. Statement0
   c. Undefined
   d. Undefined

Chapter 6. Integration

36. A _____ is a set of numbers that designate location in a given reference system, such as x,y in a planar _____ system or an x,y,z in a three-dimensional _____ system.
    a. Coordinate0
    b. Thing
    c. Undefined
    d. Undefined

37. In mathematics and its applications, a _____ is a system for assigning an n-tuple of numbers or scalars to each point in an n-dimensional space.
    a. Coordinate system0
    b. Concept
    c. Undefined
    d. Undefined

38. _____ are activities that are governed by a set of rules or customs and often engaged in competitively.
    a. Sports0
    b. Thing
    c. Undefined
    d. Undefined

39. In mathematics, an _____, mean, or central tendency of a data set refers to a measure of the "middle" or "expected" value of the data set.
    a. Average0
    b. Concept
    c. Undefined
    d. Undefined

40. _____ is the application of tools and a processing medium to the transformation of raw materials into finished goods for sale.
    a. Manufacturing0
    b. Thing
    c. Undefined
    d. Undefined

41. _____ is the extra revenue that an additional unit of product will bring a firm. It can also be described as the change in total revenue/change in number of units sold.
    a. Thing
    b. Marginal revenue0
    c. Undefined
    d. Undefined

42. _____ is a business term for the amount of money that a company receives from its activities in a given period, mostly from sales of products and/or services to customers
    a. Revenue0
    b. Thing
    c. Undefined
    d. Undefined

43. In economics, supply and _____ describe market relations between prospective sellers and buyers of a good.
    a. Thing
    b. Demand0
    c. Undefined
    d. Undefined

44. In the scientific method, an _____ (Latin: ex-+-periri, "of (or from) trying"), is a set of actions and observations, performed in the context of solving a particular problem or question, in order to support or falsify a hypothesis or research concerning phenomena.
    a. Thing
    b. Experiment0
    c. Undefined
    d. Undefined

45. A _____ function is a function for which, intuitively, small changes in the input result in small changes in the output.

a. Continuous0
b. Event
c. Undefined
d. Undefined

46. In calculus, the _____ is a formula for the derivative of the composite of two functions.
    a. Concept
    b. Chain rule0
    c. Undefined
    d. Undefined

47. An _____ is a combination of numbers, operators, grouping symbols and/or free variables and bound variables arranged in a meaningful way which can be evaluated..
    a. Expression0
    b. Thing
    c. Undefined
    d. Undefined

48. _____ is a tool for finding antiderivatives and integrals. Using the fundamental theorem of calculus often requires finding an antiderivative. For this and other reasons, this rule is a relatively important tool for mathematicians. It is the counterpart to the chain rule of differentiation.
    a. Integration by substitution0
    b. Thing
    c. Undefined
    d. Undefined

49. A _____ is traditionally an infinitesimally small change in a variable.
    a. Differential0
    b. Thing
    c. Undefined
    d. Undefined

50. In mathematics, factorization (British English: factorisation) or factoring is the decomposition of an object (for example, a number, a polynomial, or a matrix) into a product of other objects, or _____, which when multiplied together give the original.
    a. Factors0
    b. Thing
    c. Undefined
    d. Undefined

51. The _____ is used to discard one of the variables in an equation, only to replace it with the actual value when solving multiple equations.
    a. Substitution method0
    b. Thing
    c. Undefined
    d. Undefined

52. A _____ is a negotiable instrument instructing a financial institution to pay a specific amount of a specific currency from a specific demand account held in the maker/depositor's name with that institution. Both the maker and payee may be natural persons or legal entities.
    a. Check0
    b. Thing
    c. Undefined
    d. Undefined

53. _____, a field in mathematics, is the study of how functions change when their inputs change. The primary object of study in _____ is the derivative.
    a. Differential calculus0
    b. Thing
    c. Undefined
    d. Undefined

54. In mathematics, the conjugate _____ or adjoint matrix of an m-by-n matrix A with complex entries is the n-by-m matrix A* obtained from A by taking the transpose and then taking the complex conjugate of each entry.

Chapter 6. Integration

a. Pairs0
b. Thing
c. Undefined
d. Undefined

55. _____ are expenses whose total does not change in proportion to the activity of a business, within the relevant time period or scale of production
    a. Thing
    b. Fixed costs0
    c. Undefined
    d. Undefined

56. Acid _____ ratio measures the ability of a company to use its near cash or quick assets to immediately extinguish its current liabilities.
    a. Thing
    b. Test0
    c. Undefined
    d. Undefined

57. In plane geometry, a _____ is a polygon with four equal sides, four right angles, and parallel opposite sides. In algebra, the _____ of a number is that number multiplied by itself.
    a. Thing
    b. Square0
    c. Undefined
    d. Undefined

58. Initial objects are also called _____, and terminal objects are also called final.
    a. Thing
    b. Coterminal0
    c. Undefined
    d. Undefined

59. _____ is a synonym for information.
    a. Thing
    b. Data0
    c. Undefined
    d. Undefined

60. In classical geometry, a _____ of a circle or sphere is any line segment from its center to its boundary. By extension, the _____ of a circle or sphere is the length of any such segment. The _____ is half the diameter. In science and engineering the term _____ of curvature is commonly used as a synonym for _____.
    a. Thing
    b. Radius0
    c. Undefined
    d. Undefined

61. _____ are a measure of time.
    a. Thing
    b. Minutes0
    c. Undefined
    d. Undefined

62. A _____ is a mathematical equation for an unknown function of one or several variables which relates the values of the function itself and of its derivatives of various orders.
    a. Differential equation0
    b. Thing
    c. Undefined
    d. Undefined

63. A _____ is a graphical tool to qualitatively visualize, or aid in numerical approximation of, solutions to differential equations.
    a. Slope field0
    b. Thing
    c. Undefined
    d. Undefined

Chapter 6. Integration

64. In geometry, a line _____ is a part of a line that is bounded by two end points, and contains every point on the line between its end points.
    a. Concept
    b. Segment0
    c. Undefined
    d. Undefined

65. In trigonometry, the _____ is a function defined as $\tan x = \sin x / \cos x$. The function is so-named because it can be defined as the length of a certain segment of a _____ (in the geometric sense) to the unit circle. In plane geometry, a line is _____ to a curve, at some point, if both line and curve pass through the point with the same direction.
    a. Thing
    b. Tangent0
    c. Undefined
    d. Undefined

66. _____ has two distinct but etymologically-related meanings: one in geometry and one in trigonometry.
    a. Thing
    b. Tangent line0
    c. Undefined
    d. Undefined

67. A _____ is a part of a line that is bounded by two end points, and contains every point on the line between its end points.
    a. Line segment0
    b. Thing
    c. Undefined
    d. Undefined

68. _____ is a kind of property which exists as magnitude or multitude. It is among the basic classes of things along with quality, substance, change, and relation.
    a. Amount0
    b. Thing
    c. Undefined
    d. Undefined

69. _____ is the fee paid on borrowed money.
    a. Thing
    b. Interest0
    c. Undefined
    d. Undefined

70. _____ interest refers to the fact that whenever interest is calculated, it is based not only on the original principal, but also on any unpaid interest that has been added to the principal.
    a. Thing
    b. Compound0
    c. Undefined
    d. Undefined

71. _____ refers to the fact that whenever interest is calculated, it is based not only on the original principal, but also on any unpaid interest that has been added to the principal. The more frequently interest is compounded, the faster the balance grows.
    a. Compound interest0
    b. Concept
    c. Undefined
    d. Undefined

72. _____ generally derives from name. A _____ quantity e.g., length, diameter, volume, voltage, value is generally the quantity according to which some item has been named or is generally referred to.
    a. Nominal0
    b. Thing
    c. Undefined
    d. Undefined

73. Equivalence is the condition of being _____ or essentially equal.

Chapter 6. Integration

a. Thing
c. Undefined
b. Equivalent0
d. Undefined

74. _____ is a mathematical operation, written a^n, involving two numbers, the base a and the exponent n.
a. Exponentiating0
c. Undefined
b. Thing
d. Undefined

75. _____ is a mathematical operation, written a^n, involving two numbers, the base a and the exponent n.
a. Thing
c. Undefined
b. Exponentiation0
d. Undefined

76. In mathematics, two quantities are called _____ if they vary in such a way that one of the quantities is a constant multiple of the other, or equivalently if they have a constant ratio.
a. Proportional0
c. Undefined
b. Thing
d. Undefined

77. In mathematics, _____ occurs when the growth rate of a function is always proportional to the function's current size.
a. Exponential growth0
c. Undefined
b. Thing
d. Undefined

78. _____ is the process in which an unstable atomic nucleus loses energy by emitting radiation in the form of particles or electromagnetic waves.
a. Thing
c. Undefined
b. Radioactive decay0
d. Undefined

79. The _____ is the period of time required for a quantity to double in size or value.
a. Thing
c. Undefined
b. Doubling time0
d. Undefined

80. In epidemiology, an _____ is a disease that appears as new cases in a given human population, during a given period, at a rate that substantially exceeds with is "expected," based on recent experience.
a. Thing
c. Undefined
b. Epidemic0
d. Undefined

81. _____ is a decrease that follows an exponential function.
a. Exponential decay0
c. Undefined
b. Thing
d. Undefined

82. _____ is electromagnetic radiation with a wavelength that is visible to the eye (visible _____) or, in a technical or scientific context, electromagnetic radiation of any wavelength.
a. Thing
c. Undefined
b. Light0
d. Undefined

83. In geometry, an _____ of a triangle is a straight line through a vertex and perpendicular to (i.e. forming a right angle with) the opposite side or an extension of the opposite side.

a. Altitude0
b. Concept
c. Undefined
d. Undefined

84. _____ is a term used in accounting, economics and finance with reference to the fact that assets with finite lives lose value over time.
   a. Depreciation0
   b. Thing
   c. Undefined
   d. Undefined

85. The _____ is the total number of human beings alive on the planet Earth at a given time.
   a. Thing
   b. World population0
   c. Undefined
   d. Undefined

86. A _____ is an abstract model that uses mathematical language to describe the behavior of a system. Eykhoff defined a _____ as 'a representation of the essential aspects of an existing system which presents knowledge of that system in usable form'.
   a. Mathematical model0
   b. Thing
   c. Undefined
   d. Undefined

87. In mathematics and logic, a _____ proof is a way of showing the truth or falsehood of a given statement by a straightforward combination of established facts, usually existing lemmas and theorems, without making any further assumptions.
   a. Direct0
   b. Thing
   c. Undefined
   d. Undefined

88. A _____ is 360° or 2∂ radians.
   a. Thing
   b. Turn0
   c. Undefined
   d. Undefined

89. In mathematics, a _____ is a two-dimensional manifold or surface that is perfectly flat.
   a. Thing
   b. Plane0
   c. Undefined
   d. Undefined

90. _____ is a special mathematical relationship between two quantities. Two quantities are called proportional if they vary in such a way that one of the quantities is a constant multiple of the other, or equivalently if they have a constant ratio.
   a. Thing
   b. Proportionality0
   c. Undefined
   d. Undefined

91. A _____ is the result of the addition of a set of numbers. The numbers may be natural numbers, complex numbers, matrices, or still more complicated objects. An infinite _____ is a subtle procedure known as a series.
   a. Sum0
   b. Thing
   c. Undefined
   d. Undefined

92. In geometry, a _____ is defined as a quadrilateral where all four of its angles are right angles.

Chapter 6. Integration

    a. Rectangle0
    b. Thing
    c. Undefined
    d. Undefined

93. An _____ is a straight line around which a geometric figure can be rotated.
    a. Axis0
    b. Thing
    c. Undefined
    d. Undefined

94. In mathematics, functions between ordered sets are _____ or monotone, or even isotone if they preserve the given order.
    a. Monotonic0
    b. Thing
    c. Undefined
    d. Undefined

95. Mathematical _____ is used to represent ideas.
    a. Thing
    b. Notation0
    c. Undefined
    d. Undefined

96. In mathematics, a _____ is the end result of a division problem. It can also be expressed as the number of times the divisor divides into the dividend.
    a. Quotient0
    b. Thing
    c. Undefined
    d. Undefined

97. An _____ is an increase, either of some fixed amount, for example added regularly, or of a variable amount.
    a. Increment0
    b. Thing
    c. Undefined
    d. Undefined

98. The function difference divided by the point difference is known as the _____
    a. Difference quotient0
    b. Thing
    c. Undefined
    d. Undefined

99. _____ is an adjective usually refering to being in the centre.
    a. Central0
    b. Thing
    c. Undefined
    d. Undefined

100. _____, Greek for "knowledge of nature," is the branch of science concerned with the discovery and characterization of universal laws which govern matter, energy, space, and time.
    a. Thing
    b. Physics0
    c. Undefined
    d. Undefined

101. In mathematics, an _____ is a statement about the relative size or order of two objects.
    a. Inequality0
    b. Thing
    c. Undefined
    d. Undefined

102. In topology and related areas of mathematics a _____ or Moore-Smith sequence is a generalization of a sequence, intended to unify the various notions of limit and generalize them to arbitrary topological spaces.

a. Thing
c. Undefined
b. Net0
d. Undefined

103. _____ is the transport of people on a trip/journey or the process or time involved in a person or object moving from one location to another.
a. Thing
c. Undefined
b. Travel0
d. Undefined

104. In mathematics, an inequality is a statement about the relative size or order of two objects. For example 14 > 10, or 14 is _____ 10.
a. Thing
c. Undefined
b. Greater than0
d. Undefined

105. _____ is a function whose values do not vary and thus are constant.
a. Thing
c. Undefined
b. Constant function0
d. Undefined

106. _____ is the estimation of a physical quantity such as distance, energy, temperature, or time.
a. Thing
c. Undefined
b. Measurement0
d. Undefined

107. A _____ is a unit of length, usually used to measure distance, in a number of different systems, including Imperial units, United States customary units and Norwegian/Swedish mil. Its size can vary from system to system, but in each is between 1 and 10 kilometers. In contemporary English contexts _____ refers to either:
a. Thing
c. Undefined
b. Mile0
d. Undefined

108. _____ is a unit of speed, expressing the number of international miles covered per hour.
a. Miles per hour0
c. Undefined
b. Thing
d. Undefined

109. _____ are objects, characters, or other concrete representations of ideas, concepts, or other abstractions.
a. Symbols0
c. Undefined
b. Thing
d. Undefined

110. In mathematical logic, a Gödel numbering (or Gödel _____) is a function that assigns to each symbol and well-formed formula of some formal language a unique natural number called its Gödel number.
a. Code0
c. Undefined
b. Thing
d. Undefined

111. In geometry, an _____ is a point at which a line segment or ray terminates.
a. Endpoint0
c. Undefined
b. Thing
d. Undefined

112. _____ is the middle point of a line segment.

Chapter 6. Integration

a. Thing
b. Midpoint0
c. Undefined
d. Undefined

113. _____, from Latin meaning "to make progress", is defined in two different ways. Pure economic _____ is the increase in wealth that an investor has from making an investment, taking into consideration all costs associated with that investment including the opportunity cost of capital.
a. Profit0
b. Thing
c. Undefined
d. Undefined

114. A _____ is a function for which, intuitively, small changes in the input result in small changes in the output.
a. Event
b. Continuous function0
c. Undefined
d. Undefined

115. _____ is a physical property of a system that underlies the common notions of hot and cold; something that is hotter has the greater _____.
a. Temperature0
b. Thing
c. Undefined
d. Undefined

116. _____ is a mathematical subject that includes the study of limits, derivatives, integrals, and power series and constitutes a major part of modern university curriculum.
a. Calculus0
b. Thing
c. Undefined
d. Undefined

117. In number theory, the _____ of arithmetic (or unique factorization theorem) states that every natural number greater than 1 can be written as a unique product of prime numbers.
a. Fundamental theorem0
b. Concept
c. Undefined
d. Undefined

118. _____ of calculus is the statement that the two central operations of calculus, differentiation and integration, are inverse operations: if a continuous function is first integrated and then differentiated, the original function is retrieved.
a. Fundamental Theorem of Calculus0
b. Thing
c. Undefined
d. Undefined

119. A _____ is a deliberate process for transforming one or more inputs into one or more results.
a. Calculation0
b. Thing
c. Undefined
d. Undefined

120. _____ constitutes a broad family of algorithms for calculating the numerical value of a definite integral, and by extension, the term is also sometimes used to describe the numerical solution of differential equations.
a. Thing
b. Numerical integration0
c. Undefined
d. Undefined

121. _____ is a list of goods and materials, or those goods and materials themselves, held available in stock by a business

a. Thing
b. Inventory0
c. Undefined
d. Undefined

122. In business, particularly accounting, a _____ is the time intervals that the accounts, statement, payments, or other calculations cover.
a. Thing
b. Period0
c. Undefined
d. Undefined

123. The _____ of a solid object is the three-dimensional concept of how much space it occupies, often quantified numerically.
a. Volume0
b. Thing
c. Undefined
d. Undefined

124. An _____ of a product of sums expresses it as a sum of products by using the fact that multiplication distributes over addition.
a. Expansion0
b. Thing
c. Undefined
d. Undefined

125. _____ of a population is the number of childbirths per 1,000 persons per year
a. Birth rate0
b. Thing
c. Undefined
d. Undefined

126. A _____ is a vehicle, missile or aircraft which obtains thrust by the reaction to the ejection of fast moving fluid from within a _____ engine.
a. Rocket0
b. Thing
c. Undefined
d. Undefined

127. In mathematics, especially in order theory, an _____ of a subset S of some partially ordered set is an element of P which is greater than or equal to every element of S.
a. Upper bound0
b. Thing
c. Undefined
d. Undefined

128. The word _____ comes from the Latin word linearis, which means created by lines.
a. Thing
b. Linear0
c. Undefined
d. Undefined

129. U.S. liquid _____ is legally defined as 231 cubic inches, and is equal to 3.785411784 litres or abotu 0.13368 cubic feet. This is the most common definition of a _____. The U.S. fluid ounce is defined as 1/128 of a U.S. _____.
a. Gallon0
b. Thing
c. Undefined
d. Undefined

130. A _____ is a quadrilateral, which is defined as a shape with four sides, which has a pair of parallel sides.
a. Trapezoid0
b. Thing
c. Undefined
d. Undefined

Chapter 6. Integration

131. The _____ function (weight function) is a mathematical device used when performing a sum, integral, or average in order to give some elements more of a "weight" than others.
   a. Weighted0
   b. Thing
   c. Undefined
   d. Undefined

132. A _____ is often used in statistics.
   a. Thing
   b. Weighted mean0
   c. Undefined
   d. Undefined

133. In mathematics, there are several meanings of _____ depending on the subject.
   a. Degree0
   b. Thing
   c. Undefined
   d. Undefined

134. In mathematics, a _____ is an expression that is constructed from one or more variables and constants, using only the operations of addition, subtraction, multiplication, and constant positive whole number exponents. is a _____. Note in particular that division by an expression containing a variable is not in general allowed in polynomials. [1]
   a. Thing
   b. Polynomial0
   c. Undefined
   d. Undefined

135. _____ is the chance that something is likely to happen or be the case.
   a. Thing
   b. Probability0
   c. Undefined
   d. Undefined

136. _____ is a function that represents a probability distribution in terms of integrals.
   a. Probability density function0
   b. Thing
   c. Undefined
   d. Undefined

137. _____ is mass m per unit volume V.
   a. Density0
   b. Thing
   c. Undefined
   d. Undefined

Chapter 7. Additional Integration Topics

1. In mathematics, the concept of a _____ tries to capture the intuitive idea of a geometrical one-dimensional and continuous object. A simple example is the circle.
   a. Thing
   b. Curve0
   c. Undefined
   d. Undefined

2. An _____ is a straight line around which a geometric figure can be rotated.
   a. Axis0
   b. Thing
   c. Undefined
   d. Undefined

3. In mathematics, the _____ f is the collection of all ordered pairs . In particular, graph means the graphical representation of this collection, in the form of a curve or surface, together with axes, etc. Graphing on a Cartesian plane is sometimes referred to as curve sketching.
   a. Thing
   b. Graph of a function0
   c. Undefined
   d. Undefined

4. The mathematical concept of a _____ expresses the intuitive idea of deterministic dependence between two quantities, one of which is viewed as primary and the other as secondary. A _____ then is a way to associate a unique output for each input of a specified type, for example, a real number or an element of a given set.
   a. Thing
   b. Function0
   c. Undefined
   d. Undefined

5. In elementary algebra, an _____ is a set that contains every real number between two indicated numbers and may contain the two numbers themselves.
   a. Interval0
   b. Thing
   c. Undefined
   d. Undefined

6. A _____ is a set of numbers that designate location in a given reference system, such as x,y in a planar _____ system or an x,y,z in a three-dimensional _____ system.
   a. Thing
   b. Coordinate0
   c. Undefined
   d. Undefined

7. In mathematics and its applications, a _____ is a system for assigning an n-tuple of numbers or scalars to each point in an n-dimensional space.
   a. Coordinate system0
   b. Concept
   c. Undefined
   d. Undefined

8. In mathematics, a _____ is the result of multiplying, or an expression that identifies factors to be multiplied.
   a. Thing
   b. Product0
   c. Undefined
   d. Undefined

9. In geometry, a _____ is defined as a quadrilateral where all four of its angles are right angles.
   a. Rectangle0
   b. Thing
   c. Undefined
   d. Undefined

10. In mathematical analysis and related areas of mathematics, a set is called _____, if it is, in a certain sense, of finite size.

Chapter 7. Additional Integration Topics

a. Bounded0
b. Thing
c. Undefined
d. Undefined

11. A _____ function is a function for which, intuitively, small changes in the input result in small changes in the output.
a. Event
b. Continuous0
c. Undefined
d. Undefined

12. _____ are the basic objects of study in graph theory. Informally speaking, a graph is a set of objects called points, nodes, or vertices connected by links called lines or edges.
a. Thing
b. Graphs0
c. Undefined
d. Undefined

13. A _____ is the result of the addition of a set of numbers. The numbers may be natural numbers, complex numbers, matrices, or still more complicated objects. An infinite _____ is a subtle procedure known as a series.
a. Thing
b. Sum0
c. Undefined
d. Undefined

14. In mathematics, _____ are the intuitive idea of a geometrical one-dimensional and continuous object.
a. Thing
b. Curves0
c. Undefined
d. Undefined

15. The _____ of a function is an extension of the concept of a sum, and are identified or found through the use of integration.
a. Integral0
b. Thing
c. Undefined
d. Undefined

16. _____ is a method for approximating the values of integrals.
a. Thing
b. Riemann sum0
c. Undefined
d. Undefined

17. In mathematics, the _____ of two sets A and B is the set that contains all elements of A that also belong to B (or equivalently, all elements of B that also belong to A), but no other elements.
a. Intersection0
b. Thing
c. Undefined
d. Undefined

18. A _____ is a negotiable instrument instructing a financial institution to pay a specific amount of a specific currency from a specific demand account held in the maker/depositor's name with that institution. Both the maker and payee may be natural persons or legal entities.
a. Check0
b. Thing
c. Undefined
d. Undefined

19. _____ is an extension of the concept of a sum.
a. Definite integral0
b. Thing
c. Undefined
d. Undefined

Chapter 7. Additional Integration Topics

20. _____ constitutes a broad family of algorithms for calculating the numerical value of a definite integral, and by extension, the term is also sometimes used to describe the numerical solution of differential equations.
    a. Thing
    b. Numerical integration0
    c. Undefined
    d. Undefined

21. _____ is a process of combining or accumulating. It may also refer to:
    a. Thing
    b. Integration0
    c. Undefined
    d. Undefined

22. _____ is a synonym for information.
    a. Thing
    b. Data0
    c. Undefined
    d. Undefined

23. In mathematical analysis, _____ are objects which generalize functions and probability distributions.
    a. Thing
    b. Distribution0
    c. Undefined
    d. Undefined

24. Two mathematical objects are equal if and only if they are precisely the same in every way. This defines a binary relation, _____, denoted by the sign of _____ "=" in such a way that the statement "x = y" means that x and y are equal.
    a. Equality0
    b. Thing
    c. Undefined
    d. Undefined

25. A _____ is one of the basic shapes of geometry: a polygon with three vertices and three sides which are straight line segments.
    a. Thing
    b. Triangle0
    c. Undefined
    d. Undefined

26. A _____ is a quantity that denotes the proportional amount or magnitude of one quantity relative to another.
    a. Thing
    b. Ratio0
    c. Undefined
    d. Undefined

27. The word _____ is used in a variety of ways in mathematics.
    a. Index0
    b. Thing
    c. Undefined
    d. Undefined

28. In mathematics, an _____ is a statement about the relative size or order of two objects.
    a. Inequality0
    b. Thing
    c. Undefined
    d. Undefined

29. A _____ is a function that assigns a number to subsets of a given set.
    a. Measure0
    b. Thing
    c. Undefined
    d. Undefined

30. A _____ is a special kind of ratio, indicating a relationship between two measurements with different units, such as miles to gallons or cents to pounds.

Chapter 7. Additional Integration Topics

a. Rate0
b. Thing
c. Undefined
d. Undefined

31. _____ are economic entities that give rise to future economic benefit and is controlled by the entity as a result of past transaction or other events
   a. Asset0
   b. Thing
   c. Undefined
   d. Undefined

32. In economics, supply and _____ describe market relations between prospective sellers and buyers of a good.
   a. Demand0
   b. Thing
   c. Undefined
   d. Undefined

33. In the scientific method, an _____ (Latin: ex-+-periri, "of (or from) trying"), is a set of actions and observations, performed in the context of solving a particular problem or question, in order to support or falsify a hypothesis or research concerning phenomena.
   a. Experiment0
   b. Thing
   c. Undefined
   d. Undefined

34. In mathematics, two quantities are called _____ if they vary in such a way that one of the quantities is a constant multiple of the other, or equivalently if they have a constant ratio.
   a. Proportional0
   b. Thing
   c. Undefined
   d. Undefined

35. In mathematics, an _____, mean, or central tendency of a data set refers to a measure of the "middle" or "expected" value of the data set.
   a. Average0
   b. Concept
   c. Undefined
   d. Undefined

36. _____ is the chance that something is likely to happen or be the case.
   a. Thing
   b. Probability0
   c. Undefined
   d. Undefined

37. _____ is a function that represents a probability distribution in terms of integrals.
   a. Probability density function0
   b. Thing
   c. Undefined
   d. Undefined

38. A _____ is an individual or household that purchases and uses goods and services generated within the economy.
   a. Consumer0
   b. Thing
   c. Undefined
   d. Undefined

39. _____ is a regular and continuing flow of money generated by a business or investment
   a. Thing
   b. Income stream0
   c. Undefined
   d. Undefined

40. _____ is mass m per unit volume V.

Chapter 7. Additional Integration Topics

a. Density0
c. Undefined
b. Thing
d. Undefined

41. An _____ is the limit of a definite integral, as an endpoint of the interval of integration approaches either a specified real number or ‡ or − ‡ or, in some cases, as both endpoints approach limits.
   a. Improper integral0
   b. Thing
   c. Undefined
   d. Undefined

42. A _____ is a symbolic representation denoting a quantity or expression. It often represents an "unknown" quantity that has the potential to change.
   a. Variable0
   b. Thing
   c. Undefined
   d. Undefined

43. _____ is a quantity whose values are random and to which a probability distribution is assigned.
   a. Thing
   b. Random variable0
   c. Undefined
   d. Undefined

44. In mathematics, an _____ is any of the arguments, i.e. "inputs", to a function. Thus if we have a function f(x), then x is a _____.
   a. Independent variable0
   b. Thing
   c. Undefined
   d. Undefined

45. _____ are a measure of time.
   a. Minutes0
   b. Thing
   c. Undefined
   d. Undefined

46. The _____, the average in everyday English, which is also called the arithmetic _____ (and is distinguished from the geometric _____ or harmonic _____). The average is also called the sample _____. The expected value of a random variable, which is also called the population _____.
   a. Mean0
   b. Thing
   c. Undefined
   d. Undefined

47. A _____ is a function for which, intuitively, small changes in the input result in small changes in the output.
   a. Event
   b. Continuous function0
   c. Undefined
   d. Undefined

48. In mathematics and the mathematical sciences, a _____ is a fixed, but possibly unspecified, value. This is in contrast to a variable, which is not fixed.
   a. Thing
   b. Constant0
   c. Undefined
   d. Undefined

49. _____ measures the nominal future sum of money that a given sum of money is "worth" at a specified time in the future assuming a certain interest rate; this value does not include corrections for inflation or other factors that affect the true value of money in the future.

Chapter 7. Additional Integration Topics

a. Thing
c. Undefined
b. Future value0
d. Undefined

50. _____ is the fee paid on borrowed money.
a. Interest0
c. Undefined
b. Thing
d. Undefined

51. In business, particularly accounting, a _____ is the time intervals that the accounts, statement, payments, or other calculations cover.
a. Thing
c. Undefined
b. Period0
d. Undefined

52. An _____ is the fee paid on borrow money.
a. Concept
c. Undefined
b. Interest rate0
d. Undefined

53. The _____ of measurement are a globally standardized and modernized form of the metric system.
a. Units0
c. Undefined
b. Thing
d. Undefined

54. _____ can be defined as the graph depicting the relationship between the price of a certain commodity, and the amount of it that consumers are willing and able to purchase at that given price demand.
a. Demand curve0
c. Undefined
b. Thing
d. Undefined

55. In economics, economic _____ is simply a state of the world where economic forces are balanced and in the absence of external influences the values of economic variables will not change.
a. Thing
c. Undefined
b. Equilibrium0
d. Undefined

56. _____ is the price at which the quantity demanded of a good or service is equal to the quantity supplied.
a. Equilibrium price0
c. Undefined
b. Thing
d. Undefined

57. _____ or investing is a term with several closely-related meanings in business management, finance and economics, related to saving or deferring consumption.
a. Investment0
c. Undefined
b. Thing
d. Undefined

58. Initial objects are also called _____, and terminal objects are also called final.
a. Thing
c. Undefined
b. Coterminal0
d. Undefined

59. _____ of a single or multiple future payments is the nominal amounts of money to change hands at some future date, discounted to account for the time value of money, and other factors such as investment risk.

a. Present value0 b. Thing
c. Undefined d. Undefined

60. The word _____ comes from the Latin word linearis, which means created by lines.
a. Linear0 b. Thing
c. Undefined d. Undefined

61. _____ is a regression method that models the relationship between a dependent variable Y, independent variables Xp, and a random term à.
a. Thing b. Linear regression0
c. Undefined d. Undefined

62. An _____ of a function f is a function F whose derivative is equal to f, i.e., F' = f.
a. Antiderivative0 b. Thing
c. Undefined d. Undefined

63. The _____ is a measurement of how a function changes when the values of its inputs change.
a. Derivative0 b. Thing
c. Undefined d. Undefined

64. _____ is a function that extends the concept of an ordinary sum
a. Integrand0 b. Thing
c. Undefined d. Undefined

65. _____ is the logarithm to the base e, where e is an irrational constant approximately equal to 2.718281828459.
a. Natural logarithm0 b. Thing
c. Undefined d. Undefined

66. In mathematics, a _____ of a number x is the exponent y of the power by such that $x = b^y$. The value used for the base b must be neither 0 nor 1, nor a root of 1 in the case of the extension to complex numbers, and is typically 10, e, or 2.
a. Logarithm0 b. Thing
c. Undefined d. Undefined

67. _____, from Latin meaning "to make progress", is defined in two different ways. Pure economic _____ is the increase in wealth that an investor has from making an investment, taking into consideration all costs associated with that investment including the opportunity cost of capital.
a. Thing b. Profit0
c. Undefined d. Undefined

68. _____ is the application of tools and a processing medium to the transformation of raw materials into finished goods for sale.
a. Thing b. Manufacturing0
c. Undefined d. Undefined

69. _____ is a kind of property which exists as magnitude or multitude. It is among the basic classes of things along with quality, substance, change, and relation.

Chapter 7. Additional Integration Topics

   a. Amount0
   b. Thing
   c. Undefined
   d. Undefined

70. _____ is the extra revenue that an additional unit of product will bring a firm. It can also be described as the change in total revenue/change in number of units sold.
   a. Thing
   b. Marginal revenue0
   c. Undefined
   d. Undefined

71. _____ is a business term for the amount of money that a company receives from its activities in a given period, mostly from sales of products and/or services to customers
   a. Thing
   b. Revenue0
   c. Undefined
   d. Undefined

72. In classical geometry, a _____ of a circle or sphere is any line segment from its center to its boundary. By extension, the _____ of a circle or sphere is the length of any such segment. The _____ is half the diameter. In science and engineering the term _____ of curvature is commonly used as a synonym for _____.
   a. Thing
   b. Radius0
   c. Undefined
   d. Undefined

73. A _____ consists of one quarter of the coordinate plane.
   a. Quadrant0
   b. Thing
   c. Undefined
   d. Undefined

74. In sociology and biology a _____ is the collection of people or organisms of a particular species living in a given geographic area or space, usually measured by a census.
   a. Thing
   b. Population0
   c. Undefined
   d. Undefined

75. In mathematics, _____ growth occurs when the growth rate of a function is always proportional to the function's current size.
   a. Exponential0
   b. Thing
   c. Undefined
   d. Undefined

76. In plane geometry, a _____ is a polygon with four equal sides, four right angles, and parallel opposite sides. In algebra, the _____ of a number is that number multiplied by itself.
   a. Thing
   b. Square0
   c. Undefined
   d. Undefined

77. _____ is a concept that permeates much of inferential statistics and descriptive statistics. More properly, it is "the sum of the squared deviations".
   a. Sum of squares0
   b. Thing
   c. Undefined
   d. Undefined

78. In economics, _____ describe market relations between prospective sellers and buyers of a good.

a. Supply and demand0
c. Undefined
b. Thing
d. Undefined

79. In mathematics, a _____ set is the complement of a meager set. A meager set is one which is the countable union of nowhere dense sets.
    a. Thing
    c. Undefined
    b. Residual0
    d. Undefined

Chapter 8. Multivariable Calculus

1. A _____ is a symbolic representation denoting a quantity or expression. It often represents an "unknown" quantity that has the potential to change.
   - a. Thing
   - b. Variable0
   - c. Undefined
   - d. Undefined

2. In mathematics, an _____ is any of the arguments, i.e. "inputs", to a function. Thus if we have a function f(x), then x is a _____.
   - a. Thing
   - b. Independent variable0
   - c. Undefined
   - d. Undefined

3. The mathematical concept of a _____ expresses the intuitive idea of deterministic dependence between two quantities, one of which is viewed as primary and the other as secondary. A _____ then is a way to associate a unique output for each input of a specified type, for example, a real number or an element of a given set.
   - a. Thing
   - b. Function0
   - c. Undefined
   - d. Undefined

4. In mathematics, a _____ is the result of multiplying, or an expression that identifies factors to be multiplied.
   - a. Thing
   - b. Product0
   - c. Undefined
   - d. Undefined

5. _____ is the application of tools and a processing medium to the transformation of raw materials into finished goods for sale.
   - a. Thing
   - b. Manufacturing0
   - c. Undefined
   - d. Undefined

6. Fixed costs are expenses whose total does not change in proportion to the activity of a business. Unit fixed costs decline with volume following a retangular hyperbola as the volume of production. Variable costs by contrast change in relation to the activity of a business such as sales or production volume. Along with variable costs, fixed costs make up one of the two components of total cost. In the most simple production function total cost is equal to fixed costs plus variable costs. In accounting terminology, fixed costs will broadly include all costs which are not included in cost of goods sold, and variable costs are those captured in costs of goods sold. The implicit assumption required to make the equivalence between the accounting and economics terminology is that the accounting period is equal to the period in which fixed costs do not vary in relation to production. In practice, this equivalence does not always hold and depending on the period under consideration by management, some overhead expenses can be adjusted by management, and the specific allocation of each expense to each category will be decided under cost accounting. In business planning and management accounting, usage of the terms fixed costs, variable costs and others will often differ from usage in economics, and may depend on the intended use. For example, costs may be segregated into per unit costs fixed costs per period, and variable costs as a proportion of revenue. Capital expenditures will usually be allocated separately, and depending on the purpose, a portion may be regularly allocated to expenses as depreciation and amortization and seen as a _____ per period, or the entire amount may be considered upfront fixed costs.
   - a. Fixed cost0
   - b. Thing
   - c. Undefined
   - d. Undefined

7. _____ are expenses whose total does not change in proportion to the activity of a business, within the relevant time period or scale of production

a. Thing
b. Fixed costs0
c. Undefined
d. Undefined

8. An _____ is a collection of two not necessarily distinct objects, one of which is distinguished as the first coordinate and the other as the second coordinate.
a. Thing
b. Ordered pair0
c. Undefined
d. Undefined

9. In a function the _____, is the variable which is the value, i.e. the "output", of the function.
a. Thing
b. Dependent variable0
c. Undefined
d. Undefined

10. In mathematics, the _____ of a function is the set of all "output" values produced by that function. Given a function $f : A \to B$, the _____ of f, is defined to be the set $\{x \in B : x = f(a)$ for some $a \in A\}$.
a. Range0
b. Thing
c. Undefined
d. Undefined

11. In mathematics, the conjugate _____ or adjoint matrix of an m-by-n matrix A with complex entries is the n-by-m matrix A* obtained from A by taking the transpose and then taking the complex conjugate of each entry.
a. Pairs0
b. Thing
c. Undefined
d. Undefined

12. In mathematics, a _____ of a k-place relation $L \subseteq X_1 \times \ldots \times X_k$ is one of the sets X_j, $1 \le j \le k$. In the special case where k = 2 and $L \subseteq X_1 \times X_2$ is a function $L : X_1 \to X_2$, it is conventional to refer to X_1 as the _____ of the function and to refer to X_2 as the codomain of the function.
a. Domain0
b. Thing
c. Undefined
d. Undefined

13. In mathematics, a _____ may be described informally as a number that can be given by an infinite decimal representation.
a. Real number0
b. Thing
c. Undefined
d. Undefined

14. The _____ of measurement are a globally standardized and modernized form of the metric system.
a. Units0
b. Thing
c. Undefined
d. Undefined

15. _____ are the basic objects of study in graph theory. Informally speaking, a graph is a set of objects called points, nodes, or vertices connected by links called lines or edges.
a. Graphs0
b. Thing
c. Undefined
d. Undefined

16. A _____ is a set of numbers that designate location in a given reference system, such as x,y in a planar _____ system or an x,y,z in a three-dimensional _____ system.

Chapter 8. Multivariable Calculus

a. Coordinate0
b. Thing
c. Undefined
d. Undefined

17. In mathematics and its applications, a _____ is a system for assigning an n-tuple of numbers or scalars to each point in an n-dimensional space.
a. Coordinate system0
b. Concept
c. Undefined
d. Undefined

18. A _____ is a one-dimensional picture in which the integers are shown as specially-marked points evenly spaced on a line.
a. Thing
b. Number line0
c. Undefined
d. Undefined

19. In geometry, two lines or planes if one falls on the other in such a way as to create congruent adjacent angles. The term may be used as a noun or adjective. Thus, referring to Figure 1, the line AB is the _____ to CD through the point B.
a. Perpendicular0
b. Thing
c. Undefined
d. Undefined

20. In geometry, _____ lines are two lines that share one or more common points.
a. Thing
b. Intersecting0
c. Undefined
d. Undefined

21. In mathematics, the _____ is a conic section generated by the intersection of a right circular conical surface and a plane parallel to a generating straight line of that surface. It can also be defined as locus of points in a plane which are equidistant from a given point.
a. Thing
b. Parabola0
c. Undefined
d. Undefined

22. In mathematics, a _____ is a two-dimensional manifold or surface that is perfectly flat.
a. Thing
b. Plane0
c. Undefined
d. Undefined

23. An _____ is a straight line around which a geometric figure can be rotated.
a. Axis0
b. Thing
c. Undefined
d. Undefined

24. _____ is a quadric
a. Paraboloid0
b. Thing
c. Undefined
d. Undefined

25. A real-valued function f defined on the real line is said to have a _____ point at the point $x*$, if there exists some $\varepsilon > 0$, such that f when $x - x* < \varepsilon$.
a. Thing
b. Local maximum0
c. Undefined
d. Undefined

Chapter 8. Multivariable Calculus

26. In the most general terms, a _____ for a smooth function (curve, surface or hypersurface) is a point such that the curve/surface/etc. in the neighborhood of this point lies on different sides of the tangent at this point. In certain contexts the definition may vary. It is most frequently used at critical points.
   a. Thing
   b. Saddle point0
   c. Undefined
   d. Undefined

27. In geometry, a _____ is the intersection of a body in 2-dimensional space with a line, or of a body in 3-dimensional space with a plane
   a. Cross section0
   b. Thing
   c. Undefined
   d. Undefined

28. In mathematics, the _____ f is the collection of all ordered pairs . In particular, graph means the graphical representation of this collection, in the form of a curve or surface, together with axes, etc. Graphing on a Cartesian plane is sometimes referred to as curve sketching.
   a. Graph of a function0
   b. Thing
   c. Undefined
   d. Undefined

29. In mathematics, _____ are two-dimensional manifolds or surfaces that are perfectly flat.
   a. Planes0
   b. Thing
   c. Undefined
   d. Undefined

30. _____ are external two-dimensional outlines, with the appearance or configuration of some thing - in contrast to the matter or content or substance of which it is composed.
   a. Thing
   b. Shapes0
   c. Undefined
   d. Undefined

31. In Euclidean geometry, a _____ is the set of all points in a plane at a fixed distance, called the radius, from a given point, the center.
   a. Thing
   b. Circle0
   c. Undefined
   d. Undefined

32. In classical geometry, a _____ of a circle or sphere is any line segment from its center to its boundary. By extension, the _____ of a circle or sphere is the length of any such segment. The _____ is half the diameter. In science and engineering the term _____ of curvature is commonly used as a synonym for _____.
   a. Radius0
   b. Thing
   c. Undefined
   d. Undefined

33. In mathematics, the _____ of a coordinate system is the point where the axes of the system intersect.
   a. Thing
   b. Origin0
   c. Undefined
   d. Undefined

34. In geometry, the _____ of an object is a point in some sense in the middle of the object.
   a. Center0
   b. Thing
   c. Undefined
   d. Undefined

Chapter 8. Multivariable Calculus

35. _____ is a business term for the amount of money that a company receives from its activities in a given period, mostly from sales of products and/or services to customers
    a. Thing
    b. Revenue0
    c. Undefined
    d. Undefined

36. In economics, supply and _____ describe market relations between prospective sellers and buyers of a good.
    a. Demand0
    b. Thing
    c. Undefined
    d. Undefined

37. _____ asserts that the maximum output of a technologically-determined production process is a mathematical function of input factors of production.
    a. Production function0
    b. Thing
    c. Undefined
    d. Undefined

38. _____ is a kind of property which exists as magnitude or multitude. It is among the basic classes of things along with quality, substance, change, and relation.
    a. Amount0
    b. Thing
    c. Undefined
    d. Undefined

39. A _____ is a special kind of ratio, indicating a relationship between two measurements with different units, such as miles to gallons or cents to pounds.
    a. Rate0
    b. Thing
    c. Undefined
    d. Undefined

40. In business, particularly accounting, a _____ is the time intervals that the accounts, statement, payments, or other calculations cover.
    a. Thing
    b. Period0
    c. Undefined
    d. Undefined

41. _____ is the income from capital investment paid in a series of regular payments.
    a. Thing
    b. Annuity0
    c. Undefined
    d. Undefined

42. _____ is the fee paid on borrowed money.
    a. Thing
    b. Interest0
    c. Undefined
    d. Undefined

43. _____ measures the nominal future sum of money that a given sum of money is "worth" at a specified time in the future assuming a certain interest rate; this value does not include corrections for inflation or other factors that affect the true value of money in the future.
    a. Thing
    b. Future value0
    c. Undefined
    d. Undefined

44. The _____ of a solid object is the three-dimensional concept of how much space it occupies, often quantified numerically.

a. Thing
c. Undefined
b. Volume0
d. Undefined

45. _____ is the flow of blood in the cardiovascular system.
a. Blood flow0
c. Undefined
b. Thing
d. Undefined

46. _____ are a measure of time.
a. Minutes0
c. Undefined
b. Thing
d. Undefined

47. In mathematics and the mathematical sciences, a _____ is a fixed, but possibly unspecified, value. This is in contrast to a variable, which is not fixed.
a. Thing
c. Undefined
b. Constant0
d. Undefined

48. _____ is the ratio of the maximum width of the head to its maximum length i.e., in the horizontal plane, or front to back, sometimes multiplied by 100 for convenience.
a. Thing
c. Undefined
b. Cephalic index0
d. Undefined

49. The word _____ is used in a variety of ways in mathematics.
a. Index0
c. Undefined
b. Thing
d. Undefined

50. A _____ is a unit of length, usually used to measure distance, in a number of different systems, including Imperial units, United States customary units and Norwegian/Swedish mil. Its size can vary from system to system, but in each is between 1 and 10 kilometers. In contemporary English contexts _____ refers to either:
a. Thing
c. Undefined
b. Mile0
d. Undefined

51. _____ is a unit of speed, expressing the number of international miles covered per hour.
a. Miles per hour0
c. Undefined
b. Thing
d. Undefined

52. _____ of a function of several variables is its derivative with respect to one of those variables with the others held constant as opposed to the total derivative, in which all variables are allowed to vary.
a. Partial derivative0
c. Undefined
b. Thing
d. Undefined

53. The _____ is a measurement of how a function changes when the values of its inputs change.
a. Thing
c. Undefined
b. Derivative0
d. Undefined

Chapter 8. Multivariable Calculus

54. _____ is often used to describe the measurement of the steepness, incline, gradient, or grade of a straight line. The _____ is defined as the ratio of the "rise" divided by the "run" between two points on a line, or in other words, the ratio of the altitude change to the horizontal distance between any two points on the line.
   a. Thing
   b. Slope0
   c. Undefined
   d. Undefined

55. In trigonometry, the _____ is a function defined as $\tan x = \sin x / \cos x$. The function is so-named because it can be defined as the length of a certain segment of a _____ (in the geometric sense) to the unit circle. In plane geometry, a line is _____ to a curve, at some point, if both line and curve pass through the point with the same direction.
   a. Thing
   b. Tangent0
   c. Undefined
   d. Undefined

56. _____ has two distinct but etymologically-related meanings: one in geometry and one in trigonometry.
   a. Thing
   b. Tangent line0
   c. Undefined
   d. Undefined

57. _____, from Latin meaning "to make progress", is defined in two different ways. Pure economic _____ is the increase in wealth that an investor has from making an investment, taking into consideration all costs associated with that investment including the opportunity cost of capital.
   a. Thing
   b. Profit0
   c. Undefined
   d. Undefined

58. A pair of angles are _____ if the sum of their angles is 90°.
   a. Concept
   b. Complementary0
   c. Undefined
   d. Undefined

59. Acid _____ ratio measures the ability of a company to use its near cash or quick assets to immediately extinguish its current liabilities.
   a. Test0
   b. Thing
   c. Undefined
   d. Undefined

60. _____ has many meanings, most of which simply .
   a. Thing
   b. Power0
   c. Undefined
   d. Undefined

61. _____ is a free computer algebra system based on a 1982 version of Macsyma
   a. Maxima0
   b. Thing
   c. Undefined
   d. Undefined

62. _____ are points in the domain of a function at which the function takes a largest value or smallest value, either within a given neighborhood or on the function domain in its entirety.
   a. Maxima and minima0
   b. Thing
   c. Undefined
   d. Undefined

63. In mathematics, maxima and _____, known collectively as extrema, are points in the domain of a function at which the function takes a largest value .

Chapter 8. Multivariable Calculus

    a. Thing
    b. Minima0
    c. Undefined
    d. Undefined

64. In abstract algebra, _____ consists of sets with binary operations that satisfy certain axioms.
    a. Grouping0
    b. Thing
    c. Undefined
    d. Undefined

65. Deductive _____ is the kind of _____ in which the conclusion is necessitated by, or reached from, previously known facts (the premises).
    a. Reasoning0
    b. Thing
    c. Undefined
    d. Undefined

66. In mathematics, a _____ is a statement that can be proved on the basis of explicitly stated or previously agreed assumptions.
    a. Thing
    b. Theorem0
    c. Undefined
    d. Undefined

67. in mathematics, maxima and minima, known collectively as _____, are the largest value maximum or smallest value minimum, that a function takes in a point either within a given neighborhood or on the function domain in its entirety global extremum.
    a. Thing
    b. Extrema0
    c. Undefined
    d. Undefined

68. In mathematics, maxima and minima, known collectively as extrema, are the largest value maximum or smallest value minimum, that a function takes in a point either within a given neighborhood local _____ or on the function domain in its entirety global _____.
    a. Extremum0
    b. Thing
    c. Undefined
    d. Undefined

69. _____ Logic is a concept in traditional logic referring to a "type of immediate inference in which from a given proposition another proposition is inferred which has as its subject the predicate of the original proposition and as its predicate the subject of the original proposition (the quality of the proposition being retained)."
    a. Concept
    b. Converse0
    c. Undefined
    d. Undefined

70. _____ is a point on the domain of a function
    a. Thing
    b. Critical point0
    c. Undefined
    d. Undefined

71. A _____ of a number is the product of that number with any integer.
    a. Multiple0
    b. Thing
    c. Undefined
    d. Undefined

72. Generally, a _____ is a splitting of something into parts.

Chapter 8. Multivariable Calculus

a. Thing
b. Partition0
c. Undefined
d. Undefined

73. _____ is the state of being greater than any finite real or natural number, however large.
a. Infinite0
b. Thing
c. Undefined
d. Undefined

74. In plane geometry, a _____ is a polygon with four equal sides, four right angles, and parallel opposite sides. In algebra, the _____ of a number is that number multiplied by itself.
a. Thing
b. Square0
c. Undefined
d. Undefined

75. A _____ is the result of the addition of a set of numbers. The numbers may be natural numbers, complex numbers, matrices, or still more complicated objects. An infinite _____ is a subtle procedure known as a series.
a. Thing
b. Sum0
c. Undefined
d. Undefined

76. _____ are a method for finding the extrema of a function of several variables subject to one or more constraints: it is the basic tool in nonlinear constrained optimization.
a. Thing
b. Lagrange multipliers0
c. Undefined
d. Undefined

77. In mathematics, a _____ is a condition that a solution to an optimization problem must satisfy in order to be acceptable.
a. Thing
b. Constraint0
c. Undefined
d. Undefined

78. In mathematics, _____ expressions is used to reduce the expression into the lowest possible term.
a. Simplifying0
b. Thing
c. Undefined
d. Undefined

79. _____ is an economics theory, that refers to individuals or societies gaining the maximum amount out of the resources they have available to them.
a. Thing
b. Maximization0
c. Undefined
d. Undefined

80. The _____ or kilogramme is the SI base unit of mass. It is defined as being equal to the mass of the international prototype of the _____.
a. Thing
b. Kilogram0
c. Undefined
d. Undefined

81. In chemistry, a _____ is substance made by combining two or more different materials in such a way that no chemical reaction occurs.
a. Mixture0
b. Thing
c. Undefined
d. Undefined

Chapter 8. Multivariable Calculus

82. _____ is a synonym for information.
   a. Thing
   b. Data0
   c. Undefined
   d. Undefined

83. In regression analysis, _____, also known as ordinary _____ analysis is a method for linear regression that determines the values of unknown quantities in a statistical model by minimizing the sum of the residuals difference between the predicted and observed values squared.
   a. Thing
   b. Least squares0
   c. Undefined
   d. Undefined

84. The word _____ comes from the Latin word linearis, which means created by lines.
   a. Thing
   b. Linear0
   c. Undefined
   d. Undefined

85. A _____ is a first degree polynomial mathematical function of the form: $f(x) = mx + b$ where m and b are real constants and x is a real variable.
   a. Thing
   b. Linear function0
   c. Undefined
   d. Undefined

86. In mathematics, an _____, mean, or central tendency of a data set refers to a measure of the "middle" or "expected" value of the data set.
   a. Concept
   b. Average0
   c. Undefined
   d. Undefined

87. Mathematical _____ is used to represent ideas.
   a. Notation0
   b. Thing
   c. Undefined
   d. Undefined

88. _____ is the addition of a set of numbers; the result is their sum. The "numbers" to be summed may be natural numbers, complex numbers, matrices, or still more complicated objects. An infinite sum is a subtle procedure known as a series.
   a. Thing
   b. Summation0
   c. Undefined
   d. Undefined

89. An _____ is a combination of numbers, operators, grouping symbols and/or free variables and bound variables arranged in a meaningful way which can be evaluated..
   a. Thing
   b. Expression0
   c. Undefined
   d. Undefined

90. In mathematics, a _____ set is the complement of a meager set. A meager set is one which is the countable union of nowhere dense sets.
   a. Thing
   b. Residual0
   c. Undefined
   d. Undefined

91. _____ is a concept that permeates much of inferential statistics and descriptive statistics. More properly, it is "the sum of the squared deviations".

Chapter 8. Multivariable Calculus

a. Thing
c. Undefined
b. Sum of squares0
d. Undefined

92. In geographic information systems, a _____ comprises an entity with a geographic location, typically determined by points, arcs, or polygons. Carriageways and cadastres exemplify _____ data.
a. Thing
c. Undefined
b. Feature0
d. Undefined

93. _____ is a regression method that models the relationship between a dependent variable Y, independent variables Xp, and a random term å.
a. Thing
c. Undefined
b. Linear regression0
d. Undefined

94. In mathematics, a _____ is a mathematical statement which appears likely to be true, but has not been formally proven to be true under the rules of mathematical logic.
a. Concept
c. Undefined
b. Conjecture0
d. Undefined

95. In mathematics, a _____ is a polynomial equation of the second degree. The general form is $ax^2 + bx + c = 0$.
a. Quadratic equation0
c. Undefined
b. Thing
d. Undefined

96. A _____ is a statement or claimt that a particular event will occur in the future in more certain terms than a forecast.
a. Prediction0
c. Undefined
b. Thing
d. Undefined

97. In mathematics and elsewhere, the adjective _____ means fourth order, such as the function x4. A _____ number is a number which equals the fourth power of an integer.
a. Quartic0
c. Undefined
b. Thing
d. Undefined

98. In mathematics, _____ growth occurs when the growth rate of a function is always proportional to the function's current size.
a. Thing
c. Undefined
b. Exponential0
d. Undefined

99. In mathematics, a _____ is a constant multiplicative factor of a certain object. The object can be such things as a variable, a vector, a function, etc. For example, the _____ of $9x^2$ is 9.
a. Thing
c. Undefined
b. Coefficient0
d. Undefined

100. In a mathematical proof or a syllogism, a _____ is a statement that is the logical consequence of preceding statements.

Chapter 8. Multivariable Calculus

a. Conclusion0
b. Concept
c. Undefined
d. Undefined

101. A _____ is a polynomial function of the form $f(x) = ax^2 + bx + c$, where a, b, c are real numbers and a , 0.
   a. Event
   b. Quadratic function0
   c. Undefined
   d. Undefined

102. In the scientific method, an _____ (Latin: ex-+-periri, "of (or from) trying"), is a set of actions and observations, performed in the context of solving a particular problem or question, in order to support or falsify a hypothesis or research concerning phenomena.
   a. Experiment0
   b. Thing
   c. Undefined
   d. Undefined

103. In mathematics, _____ refers to the rewriting of an expression into a simpler form.
   a. Reduction0
   b. Thing
   c. Undefined
   d. Undefined

104. _____ is a temperature scale named after the German physicist Daniel Gabriel _____, who proposed it in 1724.
   a. Fahrenheit0
   b. Thing
   c. Undefined
   d. Undefined

105. A _____ is an equation in which each term is either a constant or the product of a constant times the first power of a variable.
   a. Thing
   b. Linear equation0
   c. Undefined
   d. Undefined

106. In mathematics, there are several meanings of _____ depending on the subject.
   a. Thing
   b. Degree0
   c. Undefined
   d. Undefined

107. _____ is a physical property of a system that underlies the common notions of hot and cold; something that is hotter has the greater _____.
   a. Temperature0
   b. Thing
   c. Undefined
   d. Undefined

108. In geometry, an _____ of a triangle is a straight line through a vertex and perpendicular to (i.e. forming a right angle with) the opposite side or an extension of the opposite side.
   a. Concept
   b. Altitude0
   c. Undefined
   d. Undefined

109. The _____ of a function is an extension of the concept of a sum, and are identified or found through the use of integration.
   a. Thing
   b. Integral0
   c. Undefined
   d. Undefined

Chapter 8. Multivariable Calculus

110. In Euclidean geometry, an _____ is a closed segment of a differentiable curve in the two-dimensional plane; for example, a circular _____ is a segment of a circle.
   a. Concept
   b. Arc0
   c. Undefined
   d. Undefined

111. A _____ is a negotiable instrument instructing a financial institution to pay a specific amount of a specific currency from a specific demand account held in the maker/depositor's name with that institution. Both the maker and payee may be natural persons or legal entities.
   a. Thing
   b. Check0
   c. Undefined
   d. Undefined

112. _____ is a process of combining or accumulating. It may also refer to:
   a. Thing
   b. Integration0
   c. Undefined
   d. Undefined

113. An _____ of a function f is a function F whose derivative is equal to f, i.e., F' = f.
   a. Thing
   b. Antiderivative0
   c. Undefined
   d. Undefined

114. _____ in calculus is primitive or indefinite integral of a function f is a function F whose derivative is equal to f, i.e., F Œ = f. The process of solving for antiderivatives is _____
   a. Antidifferentiation0
   b. Thing
   c. Undefined
   d. Undefined

115. In calculus, the indefinite integral of a given function i.e. the set of all antiderivatives of the function is always written with a constant, the _____.
   a. Constant of integration0
   b. Thing
   c. Undefined
   d. Undefined

116. _____, a field in mathematics, is the study of how functions change when their inputs change. The primary object of study in _____ is the derivative.
   a. Differential calculus0
   b. Thing
   c. Undefined
   d. Undefined

117. _____ is an extension of the concept of a sum.
   a. Definite integral0
   b. Thing
   c. Undefined
   d. Undefined

118. In geometry, a _____ is defined as a quadrilateral where all four of its angles are right angles.
   a. Rectangle0
   b. Thing
   c. Undefined
   d. Undefined

119. A _____ is the part of a fraction that tells how many equal parts make up a whole, and which is used in the name of the fraction: "halves", "thirds", "fourths" or "quarters", "fifths" and so on.

Chapter 8. Multivariable Calculus

a. Concept
b. Denominator0
c. Undefined
d. Undefined

120. In mathematics, _____ geometry was the traditional name for the geometry of three-dimensional Euclidean space — for practical purposes the kind of space we live in.
a. Solid0
b. Thing
c. Undefined
d. Undefined

121. A _____ is a deliberate process for transforming one or more inputs into one or more results.
a. Thing
b. Calculation0
c. Undefined
d. Undefined

122. A _____ signifies a point or points of probability on a subject e.g., the _____ of creativity, which allows for the formation of rule or norm or law by interpretation of the phenomena events that can be created.
a. Thing
b. Principle0
c. Undefined
d. Undefined

123. In sociology and biology a _____ is the collection of people or organisms of a particular species living in a given geographic area or space, usually measured by a census.
a. Population0
b. Thing
c. Undefined
d. Undefined

124. In mathematical analysis, _____ are objects which generalize functions and probability distributions.
a. Distribution0
b. Thing
c. Undefined
d. Undefined

125. A _____ is a function that assigns a number to subsets of a given set.
a. Measure0
b. Thing
c. Undefined
d. Undefined

126. In topology, the _____ are subsets S of a topological space X is the set of points which can be approached both from S and from the outside of S.
a. Boundaries0
b. Thing
c. Undefined
d. Undefined

127. In mathematics, a _____ is the end result of a division problem. It can also be expressed as the number of times the divisor divides into the dividend.
a. Thing
b. Quotient0
c. Undefined
d. Undefined

128. An _____ is a score derived from one of several different standardized tests attempting to measure intelligence.
a. Intelligence Quotient0
b. Thing
c. Undefined
d. Undefined

129. _____ is an adjective usually refering to being in the centre.

Chapter 8. Multivariable Calculus

a. Thing
c. Undefined

b. Central0
d. Undefined

130. _____ is a statistical measure of the average length of survival of a living thing.
a. Thing
c. Undefined

b. Life expectancy0
d. Undefined

131. In mathematics, the concept of a _____ tries to capture the intuitive idea of a geometrical one-dimensional and continuous object. A simple example is the circle.
a. Curve0
c. Undefined

b. Thing
d. Undefined

132. In mathematics, a _____ number (or a _____) is a natural number that has exactly two (distinct) natural number divisors, which are 1 and the _____ number itself.
a. Thing
c. Undefined

b. Prime0
d. Undefined

133. The payment of _____ as remuneration for services rendered or products sold is a common way to reward sales people.
a. Commission0
c. Undefined

b. Thing
d. Undefined

134. _____ constitutes a broad family of algorithms for calculating the numerical value of a definite integral, and by extension, the term is also sometimes used to describe the numerical solution of differential equations.
a. Thing
c. Undefined

b. Numerical integration0
d. Undefined

135. In mathematics, a _____ is an expression that is constructed from one or more variables and constants, using only the operations of addition, subtraction, multiplication, and constant positive whole number exponents. is a _____. Note in particular that division by an expression containing a variable is not in general allowed in polynomials. [1]
a. Polynomial0
c. Undefined

b. Thing
d. Undefined

Chapter 9. Trigonometric Functions

1. In mathematics, the _____ functions are functions of an angle; they are important when studying triangles and modeling periodic phenomena, among many other applications.
   a. Thing
   b. Trigonometric0
   c. Undefined
   d. Undefined

2. The _____ are functions of an angle; they are important when studying triangles and modeling periodic phenomena, among many other applications.
   a. Trigonometric functions0
   b. Thing
   c. Undefined
   d. Undefined

3. _____ are objects, characters, or other concrete representations of ideas, concepts, or other abstractions.
   a. Symbols0
   b. Thing
   c. Undefined
   d. Undefined

4. In mathematics, _____ growth occurs when the growth rate of a function is always proportional to the function's current size.
   a. Exponential0
   b. Thing
   c. Undefined
   d. Undefined

5. _____ is one of the most important functions in mathematics. A function commonly used to study growth and decay
   a. Thing
   b. Exponential function0
   c. Undefined
   d. Undefined

6. _____ is a process of combining or accumulating. It may also refer to:
   a. Thing
   b. Integration0
   c. Undefined
   d. Undefined

7. In mathematics, there are several meanings of _____ depending on the subject.
   a. Thing
   b. Degree0
   c. Undefined
   d. Undefined

8. The _____ is a measurement of how a function changes when the values of its inputs change.
   a. Derivative0
   b. Thing
   c. Undefined
   d. Undefined

9. The mathematical concept of a _____ expresses the intuitive idea of deterministic dependence between two quantities, one of which is viewed as primary and the other as secondary. A _____ then is a way to associate a unique output for each input of a specified type, for example, a real number or an element of a given set.
   a. Thing
   b. Function0
   c. Undefined
   d. Undefined

10. _____ are the basic objects of study in graph theory. Informally speaking, a graph is a set of objects called points, nodes, or vertices connected by links called lines or edges.
    a. Thing
    b. Graphs0
    c. Undefined
    d. Undefined

Chapter 9. Trigonometric Functions

11. A _____, or Ocean Surface Waves are surface waves that occur in the upper layer of the ocean.
    a. Water wave0
    b. Thing
    c. Undefined
    d. Undefined

12. _____ is a kind of property which exists as magnitude or multitude. It is among the basic classes of things along with quality, substance, change, and relation.
    a. Amount0
    b. Thing
    c. Undefined
    d. Undefined

13. In geometry, an _____ is a point at which a line segment or ray terminates.
    a. Thing
    b. Endpoint0
    c. Undefined
    d. Undefined

14. A _____ given two distinct points A and B on the _____, is the set of points C on the line containing points A and B such that A is not strictly between C and B.
    a. Thing
    b. Ray0
    c. Undefined
    d. Undefined

15. In geometry, a _____ is a special kind of point, usually a corner of a polygon, polyhedron, or higher dimensional polytope. In the geometry of curves a _____ is a point of where the first derivative of curvature is zero. In graph theory, a _____ is the fundamental unit out of which graphs are formed
    a. Thing
    b. Vertex0
    c. Undefined
    d. Undefined

16. Initial objects are also called _____, and terminal objects are also called final.
    a. Thing
    b. Coterminal0
    c. Undefined
    d. Undefined

17. In mathematics, a _____ is a two-dimensional manifold or surface that is perfectly flat.
    a. Plane0
    b. Thing
    c. Undefined
    d. Undefined

18. A _____ is a movement of an object in a circular motion. A two-dimensional object rotates around a center (or point) of _____. A three-dimensional object rotates around a line called an axis. If the axis of _____ is within the body, the body is said to rotate upon itself, or spinâ€"which implies relative speed and perhaps free-movement with angular momentum. A circular motion about an external point, e.g. the Earth about the Sun, is called an orbit or more properly an orbital revolution.
    a. Rotation0
    b. Thing
    c. Undefined
    d. Undefined

19. The _____ is a unit of plane angle. It is represented by the symbol "rad" or, more rarely, by the superscript c (for "circular measure"). For example, an angle of 1.2 radians would be written "1.2 rad" or "1.2c" (second symbol can produce confusion with centigrads).
    a. Thing
    b. Radian0
    c. Undefined
    d. Undefined

20. A _____ is a function that assigns a number to subsets of a given set.
   a. Measure0
   b. Thing
   c. Undefined
   d. Undefined

21. In Euclidean geometry, an _____ is a closed segment of a differentiable curve in the two-dimensional plane; for example, a circular _____ is a segment of a circle.
   a. Arc0
   b. Concept
   c. Undefined
   d. Undefined

22. _____ is an adjective usually refering to being in the centre.
   a. Central0
   b. Thing
   c. Undefined
   d. Undefined

23. In Euclidean geometry, a _____ is the set of all points in a plane at a fixed distance, called the radius, from a given point, the center.
   a. Thing
   b. Circle0
   c. Undefined
   d. Undefined

24. The _____ is the distance around a closed curve. _____ is a kind of perimeter.
   a. Thing
   b. Circumference0
   c. Undefined
   d. Undefined

25. _____ is a unit of plane angle, equal to 180/δ degrees, or about 57.2958 degrees
   a. Radian measure0
   b. Thing
   c. Undefined
   d. Undefined

26. In classical geometry, a _____ of a circle or sphere is any line segment from its center to its boundary. By extension, the _____ of a circle or sphere is the length of any such segment. The _____ is half the diameter. In science and engineering the term _____ of curvature is commonly used as a synonym for _____.
   a. Thing
   b. Radius0
   c. Undefined
   d. Undefined

27. A _____ is a set of numbers that designate location in a given reference system, such as x,y in a planar _____ system or an x,y,z in a three-dimensional _____ system.
   a. Coordinate0
   b. Thing
   c. Undefined
   d. Undefined

28. In mathematics and its applications, a _____ is a system for assigning an n-tuple of numbers or scalars to each point in an n-dimensional space.
   a. Concept
   b. Coordinate system0
   c. Undefined
   d. Undefined

29. The _____ integers are all the integers from zero on upwards.
   a. Nonnegative0
   b. Thing
   c. Undefined
   d. Undefined

Chapter 9. Trigonometric Functions

30. An _____ is a straight line around which a geometric figure can be rotated.
    a. Axis0
    b. Thing
    c. Undefined
    d. Undefined

31. In geometry, _____, or general position for a set of points, or other configuration, means the general case situation, as opposed to some more special or coincidental cases that are possible.
    a. Standard position0
    b. Thing
    c. Undefined
    d. Undefined

32. _____ is a trigonemtric function that is important when studying triangles and modeling periodic phenomena, among other applications.
    a. Sine0
    b. Thing
    c. Undefined
    d. Undefined

33. The _____ of an angle is the ratio of the length of the adjacent side to the length of the hypotenuse.
    a. Concept
    b. Cosine0
    c. Undefined
    d. Undefined

34. An _____ is a collection of two not necessarily distinct objects, one of which is distinguished as the first coordinate and the other as the second coordinate.
    a. Ordered pair0
    b. Thing
    c. Undefined
    d. Undefined

35. The _____ is the y- coordinate of a point within a two dimensional coordinate system. It is sometimes used to refer to the axis rather than the distance along the coordinate system.
    a. Ordinate0
    b. Thing
    c. Undefined
    d. Undefined

36. In mathematics, the conjugate _____ or adjoint matrix of an m-by-n matrix A with complex entries is the n-by-m matrix A* obtained from A by taking the transpose and then taking the complex conjugate of each entry.
    a. Pairs0
    b. Thing
    c. Undefined
    d. Undefined

37. _____ consists of the first element in a coordinate pair. When graphed in the coordinate plane, it is the distance from the y-axis. Frequently called the x coordinate.
    a. Abscissa0
    b. Thing
    c. Undefined
    d. Undefined

38. In mathematics, a _____ of a k-place relation $L \subseteq X_1 \times ... \times X_k$ is one of the sets X_j, $1 \leq j \leq k$. In the special case where k = 2 and $L \subseteq X_1 \times X_2$ is a function $L : X_1 \to X_2$, it is conventional to refer to X_1 as the _____ of the function and to refer to X_2 as the codomain of the function.
    a. Thing
    b. Domain0
    c. Undefined
    d. Undefined

39. In mathematics, the _____ of a function is the set of all "output" values produced by that function. Given a function $f : A \to B$, the _____ of f, is defined to be the set $\{x \in B : x = f(a)$ for some $a \in A\}$.

a. Thing
c. Undefined
b. Range0
d. Undefined

40. In mathematics, a _____ may be described informally as a number that can be given by an infinite decimal representation.
a. Thing
c. Undefined
b. Real number0
d. Undefined

41. A _____ is a set whose members are members of another set or a set contained within another set.
a. Subset0
c. Undefined
b. Thing
d. Undefined

42. _____ is a mathematical subject that includes the study of limits, derivatives, integrals, and power series and constitutes a major part of modern university curriculum.
a. Calculus0
c. Undefined
b. Thing
d. Undefined

43. In mathematics and logic, a _____ proof is a way of showing the truth or falsehood of a given statement by a straightforward combination of established facts, usually existing lemmas and theorems, without making any further assumptions.
a. Direct0
c. Undefined
b. Thing
d. Undefined

44. _____ is the fee paid on borrowed money.
a. Thing
c. Undefined
b. Interest0
d. Undefined

45. _____ is a branch of mathematics which deals with triangles, particularly triangles in a plane where one angle of the triangle is 90 degrees, and a variety of other topological relations such as spheres, in other branches, such as spherical _____.
a. Thing
c. Undefined
b. Trigonometry0
d. Undefined

46. A _____ is a deliberate process for transforming one or more inputs into one or more results.
a. Thing
c. Undefined
b. Calculation0
d. Undefined

47. In statistics, _____ means the most frequent value assumed by a random variable, or occurring in a sampling of a random variable.
a. Mode0
c. Undefined
b. Concept
d. Undefined

48. In the scientific method, an _____ (Latin: ex-+-periri, "of (or from) trying"), is a set of actions and observations, performed in the context of solving a particular problem or question, in order to support or falsify a hypothesis or research concerning phenomena.

Chapter 9. Trigonometric Functions

a. Thing
b. Experiment0
c. Undefined
d. Undefined

49. A _____ is one of the basic shapes of geometry: a polygon with three vertices and three sides which are straight line segments.
a. Thing
b. Triangle0
c. Undefined
d. Undefined

50. A _____ of a number is the product of that number with any integer.
a. Thing
b. Multiple0
c. Undefined
d. Undefined

51. _____ is a circle with a unit radius, i.e., a circle whose radius is 1.
a. Unit circle0
b. Thing
c. Undefined
d. Undefined

52. In mathematics, the _____ of two sets A and B is the set that contains all elements of A that also belong to B (or equivalently, all elements of B that also belong to A), but no other elements.
a. Intersection0
b. Thing
c. Undefined
d. Undefined

53. In mathematics and the mathematical sciences, a _____ is a fixed, but possibly unspecified, value. This is in contrast to a variable, which is not fixed.
a. Thing
b. Constant0
c. Undefined
d. Undefined

54. In business, particularly accounting, a _____ is the time intervals that the accounts, statement, payments, or other calculations cover.
a. Period0
b. Thing
c. Undefined
d. Undefined

55. A _____ function is a function for which, intuitively, small changes in the input result in small changes in the output.
a. Event
b. Continuous0
c. Undefined
d. Undefined

56. In mathematics, the concept of a _____ tries to capture the intuitive idea of a geometrical one-dimensional and continuous object. A simple example is the circle.
a. Thing
b. Curve0
c. Undefined
d. Undefined

57. In mathematics, _____ are the intuitive idea of a geometrical one-dimensional and continuous object.
a. Curves0
b. Thing
c. Undefined
d. Undefined

58. A _____ consists of one quarter of the coordinate plane.

110   Chapter 9. Trigonometric Functions

a. Quadrant0
b. Thing
c. Undefined
d. Undefined

59. An _____ is a combination of numbers, operators, grouping symbols and/or free variables and bound variables arranged in a meaningful way which can be evaluated..
   a. Expression0
   b. Thing
   c. Undefined
   d. Undefined

60. The _____ of a solid object is the three-dimensional concept of how much space it occupies, often quantified numerically.
   a. Volume0
   b. Thing
   c. Undefined
   d. Undefined

61. _____ is a business term for the amount of money that a company receives from its activities in a given period, mostly from sales of products and/or services to customers
   a. Thing
   b. Revenue0
   c. Undefined
   d. Undefined

62. An _____ is an equality that remains true regardless of the values of any variables that appear within it, to distinguish it from an equality which is true under more particular conditions.
   a. Identity0
   b. Thing
   c. Undefined
   d. Undefined

63. _____ is often used to describe the measurement of the steepness, incline, gradient, or grade of a straight line. The _____ is defined as the ratio of the "rise" divided by the "run" between two points on a line, or in other words, the ratio of the altitude change to the horizontal distance between any two points on the line.
   a. Slope0
   b. Thing
   c. Undefined
   d. Undefined

64. _____ is a free computer algebra system based on a 1982 version of Macsyma
   a. Thing
   b. Maxima0
   c. Undefined
   d. Undefined

65. _____ are points in the domain of a function at which the function takes a largest value or smallest value, either within a given neighborhood or on the function domain in its entirety.
   a. Maxima and minima0
   b. Thing
   c. Undefined
   d. Undefined

66. The word _____ means curving in or hollowed inward.
   a. Concavity0
   b. Thing
   c. Undefined
   d. Undefined

67. In mathematics, maxima and _____, known collectively as extrema, are points in the domain of a function at which the function takes a largest value .

Chapter 9. Trigonometric Functions

a. Thing
b. Minima0
c. Undefined
d. Undefined

68. _____ is a point on the domain of a function
a. Critical point0
b. Thing
c. Undefined
d. Undefined

69. A real-valued function f defined on the real line is said to have a _____ point at the point x∗, if there exists some ε > 0, such that f when x − x∗ < ε.
a. Thing
b. Local maximum0
c. Undefined
d. Undefined

70. Any point where a graph makes contact with an coordinate axis is called an _____ of the graph
a. Thing
b. Intercept0
c. Undefined
d. Undefined

71. The _____ of a function is an extension of the concept of a sum, and are identified or found through the use of integration.
a. Thing
b. Integral0
c. Undefined
d. Undefined

72. An _____ of a function f is a function F whose derivative is equal to f, i.e., F' = f.
a. Antiderivative0
b. Thing
c. Undefined
d. Undefined

73. _____ is an extension of the concept of a sum.
a. Thing
b. Definite integral0
c. Undefined
d. Undefined

74. A _____ is a negotiable instrument instructing a financial institution to pay a specific amount of a specific currency from a specific demand account held in the maker/depositor's name with that institution. Both the maker and payee may be natural persons or legal entities.
a. Thing
b. Check0
c. Undefined
d. Undefined

75. _____ is a function that extends the concept of an ordinary sum
a. Thing
b. Integrand0
c. Undefined
d. Undefined

76. In mathematics, especially in order theory, an _____ of a subset S of some partially ordered set is an element of P which is greater than or equal to every element of S.
a. Thing
b. Upper bound0
c. Undefined
d. Undefined

77. A _____ is the result of the addition of a set of numbers. The numbers may be natural numbers, complex numbers, matrices, or still more complicated objects. An infinite _____ is a subtle procedure known as a series.

a. Thing
c. Undefined
b. Sum0
d. Undefined

78. In elementary algebra, an _____ is a set that contains every real number between two indicated numbers and may contain the two numbers themselves.
   a. Thing
   c. Undefined
   b. Interval0
   d. Undefined

79. _____ is the middle point of a line segment.
   a. Midpoint0
   c. Undefined
   b. Thing
   d. Undefined

80. _____, from Latin meaning "to make progress", is defined in two different ways. Pure economic _____ is the increase in wealth that an investor has from making an investment, taking into consideration all costs associated with that investment including the opportunity cost of capital.
   a. Thing
   c. Undefined
   b. Profit0
   d. Undefined

81. In mathematics, an _____, mean, or central tendency of a data set refers to a measure of the "middle" or "expected" value of the data set.
   a. Average0
   c. Undefined
   b. Concept
   d. Undefined

82. In mathematics, functions between ordered sets are _____ or monotone, or even isotone if they preserve the given order.
   a. Monotonic0
   c. Undefined
   b. Thing
   d. Undefined

83. _____ is a set, with some particular properties and usually some additional structure, such as the operations of addition or multiplication, for instance.
   a. Thing
   c. Undefined
   b. Space0
   d. Undefined

84. _____ is a physical property of a system that underlies the common notions of hot and cold; something that is hotter has the greater _____.
   a. Temperature0
   c. Undefined
   b. Thing
   d. Undefined

85. In economics, supply and _____ describe market relations between prospective sellers and buyers of a good.
   a. Demand0
   c. Undefined
   b. Thing
   d. Undefined

86. _____ is a mathematical science pertaining to the collection, analysis, interpretation or explanation, and presentation of data. It is applicable to a wide variety of academic disciplines, from the physical and social sciences to the humanities.

Chapter 9. Trigonometric Functions

a. Thing
c. Undefined

b. Statistics0
d. Undefined

87. In mathematics, a _____ is an expression that is constructed from one or more variables and constants, using only the operations of addition, subtraction, multiplication, and constant positive whole number exponents. is a _____. Note in particular that division by an expression containing a variable is not in general allowed in polynomials. [1]

a. Polynomial0
c. Undefined

b. Thing
d. Undefined

88. _____ constitutes a broad family of algorithms for calculating the numerical value of a definite integral, and by extension, the term is also sometimes used to describe the numerical solution of differential equations.

a. Numerical integration0
c. Undefined

b. Thing
d. Undefined

Chapter 1

1. b	2. b	3. b	4. b	5. b	6. a	7. a	8. a	9. a	10. b
11. b	12. b	13. b	14. b	15. a	16. b	17. a	18. a	19. a	20. b
21. a	22. a	23. a	24. b	25. a	26. b	27. a	28. a	29. b	30. a
31. b	32. b	33. b	34. a	35. a	36. a	37. b	38. b	39. b	40. b
41. b	42. b	43. a	44. a	45. b	46. b	47. b	48. a	49. a	50. a
51. b	52. b	53. a	54. b	55. a	56. a	57. a	58. a	59. b	60. a
61. b	62. b	63. b	64. a	65. a	66. b	67. a	68. b	69. a	70. b
71. a	72. a	73. a	74. b	75. a	76. b	77. b	78. b	79. b	80. a
81. a	82. b	83. a	84. b	85. b	86. b	87. b	88. a	89. a	90. a
91. b	92. a								

Chapter 2

1. a	2. b	3. a	4. a	5. b	6. a	7. a	8. b	9. a	10. b
11. a	12. a	13. b	14. a	15. a	16. b	17. a	18. a	19. a	20. a
21. b	22. a	23. a	24. b	25. a	26. b	27. b	28. b	29. a	30. a
31. b	32. a	33. a	34. b	35. a	36. b	37. a	38. b	39. b	40. a
41. a	42. a	43. a	44. a	45. a	46. a	47. a	48. a	49. a	50. b
51. a	52. a	53. b	54. b	55. a	56. b	57. a	58. b	59. b	60. b
61. b	62. b	63. a	64. b	65. b	66. b	67. b	68. b	69. a	70. a
71. b	72. b	73. b	74. b	75. a	76. b	77. b	78. b	79. a	80. b
81. b	82. a	83. b	84. a	85. a	86. a	87. a	88. a	89. b	90. a
91. b	92. b	93. a	94. b	95. a	96. a	97. b	98. a	99. a	100. b
101. a	102. a	103. a	104. a	105. a	106. a	107. a	108. a	109. b	110. a
111. a	112. a	113. a	114. b	115. b	116. a	117. a	118. b	119. b	120. a
121. b	122. a	123. b	124. b	125. b	126. b				

Chapter 3

1. b	2. b	3. b	4. a	5. b	6. a	7. a	8. b	9. b	10. b
11. b	12. a	13. b	14. a	15. a	16. a	17. a	18. a	19. a	20. a
21. b	22. b	23. a	24. b	25. a	26. a	27. a	28. a	29. a	30. a
31. b	32. b	33. a	34. a	35. a	36. a	37. b	38. a	39. a	40. a
41. a	42. b	43. a	44. a	45. a	46. a	47. b	48. b	49. a	50. b
51. b	52. a	53. b	54. a	55. b	56. a	57. a	58. a	59. b	60. b
61. a	62. b	63. b	64. a	65. a	66. a	67. a	68. a	69. a	70. b
71. b	72. b	73. b	74. b	75. a	76. b	77. a	78. b	79. b	80. a
81. b	82. b	83. b	84. b	85. a	86. b	87. a	88. b	89. a	90. b
91. b	92. a	93. a	94. a	95. b	96. a	97. a	98. a	99. b	100. a
101. a	102. b	103. b	104. a	105. b	106. a	107. a	108. a	109. b	110. a
111. a	112. b	113. b	114. b	115. b	116. b	117. b	118. b	119. b	120. a
121. b	122. b	123. a	124. b	125. b	126. b	127. a	128. a		

ANSWER KEY

Chapter 4

1. a	2. b	3. b	4. b	5. a	6. b	7. b	8. b	9. a	10. a
11. a	12. b	13. b	14. b	15. b	16. b	17. b	18. a	19. b	20. a
21. a	22. b	23. a	24. a	25. a	26. b	27. a	28. a	29. b	30. a
31. b	32. b	33. b	34. b	35. a	36. a	37. a	38. b	39. b	40. a
41. b	42. b	43. a	44. a	45. a	46. b	47. a	48. a	49. a	50. b
51. a	52. b	53. b	54. a	55. a	56. b	57. b	58. b	59. b	60. a
61. a	62. b	63. a	64. b	65. a	66. a	67. b	68. b	69. b	70. a
71. b	72. a	73. b	74. b	75. b	76. a	77. a	78. b	79. b	80. a
81. b	82. a	83. a	84. a	85. a	86. b	87. a	88. b	89. a	90. b
91. a	92. a	93. a	94. b	95. b	96. b	97. b	98. a	99. b	100. b
101. a	102. b	103. b	104. a	105. a	106. b	107. b	108. a	109. a	110. b
111. a	112. b	113. a	114. b	115. a	116. b	117. b	118. b	119. b	120. a
121. a	122. a	123. a	124. a	125. b	126. b	127. b	128. a	129. a	130. b
131. b	132. a	133. a	134. b	135. b	136. b	137. b			

Chapter 5

1. a	2. b	3. a	4. a	5. b	6. a	7. b	8. a	9. a	10. b
11. b	12. a	13. b	14. a	15. b	16. b	17. a	18. a	19. b	20. a
21. a	22. b	23. b	24. b	25. b	26. a	27. b	28. b	29. a	30. b
31. a	32. a	33. a	34. b	35. b	36. a	37. b	38. a	39. b	40. a
41. a	42. b	43. a	44. b	45. a	46. a	47. a	48. a	49. b	50. b
51. a	52. b	53. a	54. a	55. b	56. a	57. b	58. a	59. b	60. a
61. a	62. b	63. a	64. b	65. a	66. b	67. a	68. a	69. a	70. b
71. b	72. a	73. a	74. b	75. a	76. a	77. a	78. b	79. a	80. a
81. a	82. b	83. b	84. a	85. a	86. b	87. a	88. a	89. a	90. b
91. a	92. b	93. a	94. a	95. b	96. a				

Chapter 6

1. a	2. b	3. b	4. a	5. a	6. b	7. b	8. a	9. b	10. b
11. b	12. a	13. b	14. b	15. a	16. b	17. b	18. b	19. b	20. b
21. a	22. b	23. b	24. a	25. b	26. b	27. b	28. b	29. a	30. a
31. a	32. b	33. b	34. b	35. b	36. a	37. a	38. a	39. a	40. a
41. b	42. a	43. b	44. b	45. a	46. b	47. a	48. a	49. a	50. a
51. a	52. a	53. a	54. a	55. b	56. b	57. b	58. b	59. b	60. b
61. b	62. a	63. a	64. b	65. b	66. b	67. a	68. a	69. b	70. b
71. a	72. a	73. b	74. a	75. b	76. a	77. a	78. b	79. b	80. b
81. a	82. b	83. a	84. a	85. b	86. a	87. a	88. b	89. b	90. b
91. a	92. a	93. a	94. a	95. b	96. a	97. a	98. a	99. a	100. b
101. a	102. b	103. b	104. b	105. b	106. b	107. b	108. a	109. a	110. a
111. a	112. b	113. a	114. b	115. a	116. a	117. a	118. a	119. a	120. b
121. b	122. b	123. a	124. a	125. a	126. a	127. a	128. b	129. a	130. a
131. a	132. b	133. a	134. b	135. b	136. a	137. a			

Chapter 7

1. b	2. a	3. b	4. b	5. a	6. b	7. a	8. b	9. a	10. a
11. b	12. b	13. b	14. b	15. a	16. b	17. a	18. a	19. a	20. b
21. b	22. b	23. b	24. a	25. b	26. b	27. a	28. a	29. a	30. a
31. a	32. a	33. a	34. a	35. a	36. b	37. a	38. a	39. b	40. a
41. a	42. a	43. b	44. a	45. a	46. a	47. b	48. b	49. b	50. a
51. b	52. b	53. a	54. a	55. b	56. a	57. a	58. b	59. a	60. a
61. b	62. a	63. a	64. a	65. a	66. a	67. b	68. b	69. a	70. b
71. b	72. b	73. a	74. b	75. a	76. b	77. a	78. a	79. b	

Chapter 8

1. b	2. b	3. b	4. b	5. b	6. a	7. b	8. b	9. b	10. a
11. a	12. a	13. a	14. a	15. a	16. a	17. a	18. b	19. a	20. b
21. b	22. b	23. a	24. a	25. b	26. b	27. a	28. a	29. a	30. b
31. b	32. a	33. b	34. a	35. b	36. a	37. a	38. a	39. a	40. b
41. b	42. b	43. b	44. b	45. a	46. a	47. b	48. b	49. a	50. b
51. a	52. a	53. b	54. b	55. b	56. b	57. b	58. b	59. a	60. b
61. a	62. a	63. b	64. a	65. a	66. b	67. b	68. a	69. b	70. b
71. a	72. b	73. a	74. b	75. b	76. b	77. b	78. a	79. b	80. b
81. a	82. b	83. b	84. b	85. b	86. b	87. a	88. b	89. b	90. b
91. b	92. b	93. b	94. b	95. a	96. a	97. a	98. b	99. b	100. a
101. b	102. a	103. a	104. a	105. b	106. b	107. a	108. b	109. b	110. b
111. b	112. b	113. b	114. a	115. a	116. a	117. a	118. a	119. b	120. a
121. b	122. a	123. a	124. a	125. a	126. a	127. b	128. a	129. b	130. b
131. a	132. b	133. a	134. b	135. a					

Chapter 9

1. b	2. a	3. a	4. a	5. b	6. b	7. b	8. a	9. b	10. b
11. a	12. a	13. b	14. b	15. b	16. b	17. a	18. a	19. b	20. a
21. a	22. a	23. b	24. b	25. a	26. b	27. a	28. b	29. a	30. a
31. a	32. a	33. b	34. a	35. a	36. a	37. a	38. b	39. b	40. b
41. a	42. a	43. a	44. b	45. b	46. b	47. a	48. b	49. b	50. b
51. a	52. a	53. b	54. a	55. b	56. b	57. a	58. a	59. a	60. a
61. b	62. a	63. a	64. b	65. a	66. a	67. b	68. a	69. b	70. b
71. b	72. a	73. b	74. b	75. b	76. b	77. b	78. b	79. a	80. b
81. a	82. a	83. b	84. a	85. a	86. b	87. a	88. a		

www.ingramcontent.com/pod-product-compliance
Lightning Source LLC
Chambersburg PA
CBHW082050230426
43670CB00016B/2839